Know It, Show It

GRADE 6

Printed in the U.S.A.

ISBN 978-1-328-45338-9

4 5 6 7 8 9 10   0982   27 26 25 24 23 22 21

4500821152   A B C D E F G

Grade
6

Contents

Name _____

VCCV Syllable Division Pattern

▶ The words in the Word Bank all have the VCCV syllable division pattern. Write a word from the Word Bank that best completes each sentence. Then, draw a line to separate the two syllables in each word.

distort	plastic	suspense	oppose
garment	summit	access	skittish

1. I enjoy reading mystery books because they keep me in _____ .

2. Our new kitten is _____ and hides in the corner.

3. We have _____ to our garage from the house and from the street.

4. There are many benefits to recycling _____ .

5. The mountain climber reached the _____ .

6. Please do not ever omit information or _____ the truth.

7. The business traveler packed her clothes in a _____ bag.

8. Many students in our school _____ the new dress code.

Critical Vocabulary

You can use the words you learn from reading as you talk and write.

> Use details from *Sometimes a Dream Needs a Push* to complete the sentence stems below. Be sure to demonstrate the meaning of each Critical Vocabulary word.

1. Most modern companies give the role of an **executive** to an employee who

_____.

2. Carpenters are **equipped** with tools that help them

_____.

3. The strong **harnesses** inside a helicopter are designed to

_____.

4. In many families, dogs are seen as a **stabilizing** force because of their compassionate nature and

_____.

5. Our team **exhaled** a sigh of relief when the other team

_____.

6. The **dejected** look on the young man's face was the result of

_____.

7. The baby's **congestion** in her sinuses was causing her to

_____.

8. The **fundamentals** of being a good student include

_____.

> Choose two of the Critical Vocabulary words and use them in a sentence.

_____

_____

_____

Literary Elements

Literary elements make up a narrative. Authors may use devices such as **flashback** to help a reader learn what happened at an earlier time. Authors might organize events purposefully to drive the plot forward.

> **Answer the questions about paragraph 2 of *Sometimes a Dream Needs a Push*.**

1. What events does the narrator recall?

_____

_____

_____

2. How does the flashback support the plot?

_____

_____

_____

> **Answer the questions about paragraph 29 of *Sometimes a Dream Needs a Push*.**

3. What kind of figurative language is "The next day zoomed by"?

_____

_____

4. How do you know it is this type of figurative language?

_____

_____

5. What other word besides *zoomed* could the author have used to achieve a similar connotation?

_____

_____

Name _____

> **Answer these additional questions about *Sometimes a Dream Needs a Push.***

6. What transitional words or phrases or other clues signal that the section about the accident is a flashback?

_____

_____

_____

_____

_____

_____

7. How does the scene about the phone call with Mr. Evans in paragraphs 24–28 relate to the next scene at basketball practice?

_____

_____

_____

_____

_____

_____

Name _____

VCCV Syllable Division Pattern

▶ For each sentence below, find a word in the Word Bank that has the VCCV syllable division pattern and write it on the line. Not every word in the Word Bank has the VCCV pattern. Then, draw a line to separate the two syllables.

bandage	raccoon	contest	weed
explain	station	goblets	discuss
fungus	skunk	fractured	channel

1. The table was set with silver water _____ .

2. Trina wants to _____ our plans for the weekend after school.

3. The dog jumped off the porch to chase a squirrel and _____ its leg.

4. We have a pesky _____ in our neighborhood that loves to get into our trashcans.

5. Did you enter the art _____ at the library?

6. A mushroom is a _____ , not a vegetable.

7. Daniel likes watching the _____ dedicated to golfing events.

8. The nurse put a large _____ on my small wound.

Name _____

Prefixes ex–/e–; Latin Root miser

The prefixes *ex*– and *e*– (meaning "out of") are found in words such as **exit** and **eject**. The Latin root *miser* (meaning "wretched") is found in words such as **miserly** and **miserable**.

▶ **Complete the chart with other words that contain the prefixes *ex*– and *e*– and the Latin root *miser*.**

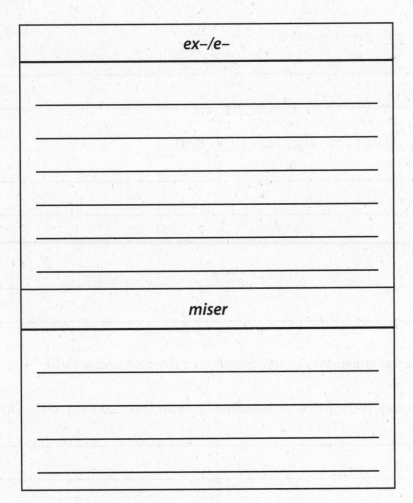

ex–/e–

_____

_____

_____

_____

_____

miser

_____

_____

_____

▶ **Write a sentence for four of the words in the chart.**

_____

_____

_____

_____

Name _____

Theme

Literature has a **theme,** or main message, that an author wants readers to know. Sometimes, a theme is clearly stated in a story. Other times, readers must infer a story's theme by analyzing the story's characters, plot, and other elements.

▶ **Answer the questions about page 28 of** *Sometimes a Dream Needs a Push.*

1. What theme can you infer in paragraph 61?

_____

_____

2. In paragraph 62, why doesn't Chris want to push his dad?

_____

_____

3. What theme does this support?

_____

_____

▶ **Answer these additional questions about** *Sometimes a Dream Needs a Push.*

4. What can you infer about the relationship between Chris and his dad early in the story?

_____

_____

5. What theme(s) can you infer about relationships after analyzing the relationship between Chris and his dad?

_____

_____

Name _____

Author's Craft

Author's craft refers to an author's use of tools and techniques of language. Author's craft makes a text easy to understand and interesting to read. **Voice** is the author's writing style and can change from one text to another. **Tone** is the author's attitude. **Mood** is the feeling or emotions that readers get while reading a text.

> **Answer the question about page 22 of** *Sometimes a Dream Needs a Push.*

1. How does the author build tension and suspense in paragraphs 11–16?

_____

_____

_____

_____

_____

_____

> **Answer the question about page 28 of** *Sometimes a Dream Needs a Push.*

2. How would you describe the tone? Cite text evidence.

_____

_____

_____

_____

_____

_____

_____

Name _____

> **Answer the questions about page 27 of *Sometimes a Dream Needs a Push*.**

3. How do word choices contribute to Chris's voice?

_____

_____

_____

_____

_____

_____

_____

4. What does sentence length tell you about Chris's voice?

_____

_____

_____

_____

_____

_____

5. What mood do you experience when you read paragraphs 55–59, and why?

_____

_____

_____

_____

_____

Name _____

VCV Syllable Division Pattern

▶ Read each sentence. The underlined word in each sentence has a VCV syllable pattern. Draw a line in each word to show where the syllables should be divided.

1. I could not open the car door because it was frozen shut.

2. Sometimes I have a craving for chocolate.

3. The witness will relate how the accident took place.

4. The medicine gave me relief from my headache.

5. Sanjeet plans to be a pilot when he grows up.

6. Anna could not locate her missing necklace.

7. This is going to be a superb party.

8. Jasper used labels to address the envelopes.

Critical Vocabulary

> Read each sentence. Underline the sentence that best fits the meaning of the word in dark print.

1. slum

Many of the houses in the crowded neighborhood had boarded-up or broken windows.

The wealthy neighborhood was full of large houses and spacious lawns.

2. principles

As I played the game more often, I developed my own strategies.

Before we set up the board game, I explained its basic rules.

3. represent

We wore matching T-shirts so everyone would know that we're friends.

Many Olympic athletes believe it's an honor to participate in a sport on behalf of their country.

> Choose one of the Critical Vocabulary words and use it in a sentence.

_____

_____

Name _____

Media Techniques

Remind students that **media techniques** are tools that are used to get messages across effectively. They may include sound elements, such as music, sound effects, and narration; they may also include visual elements, such as graphics, animation, and onscreen text.

▷ **Answer the questions about the video** *The Queen of Chess* **on page 34.**

1. What is the purpose of the subtitles, or the text displayed at the bottom of the screen?

_____

_____

2. Who are the speakers in the video? What information does each provide?

_____

_____

_____

▷ **Answer the questions about media techniques in the video** *The Queen of Chess* **on page 34.**

3. What was Phiona's life like in Uganda before chess? What details from the video's live action and narration support your response?

_____

_____

_____

4. Near the end of the video, the narrator says that chess has carried Phiona around the world. Do you agree or disagree? Cite details from the video that support your answer and discuss them with a partner.

_____

_____

15

VCV and VCCV Syllable Division Patterns

> Read each sentence. Choose one of the words from the Word Bank and write it on the line. Then, divide each word into syllables.

visor	pilot	rabbit	fever
solar	silence	viper	survive

1. A _____ is a poisonous snake.

2. Our house is heated with _____ energy.

3. My _____ has very soft fur.

4. Did you know my sister is a _____ for a major airline?

5. I usually wear a sports _____ to keep the sun off my face.

6. We walked along the riverbank in _____ , listening to the sounds of nature.

7. The hikers had enough water to _____ for three days.

8. A low-grade _____ is not dangerous, but you should see a doctor if gets over 102 degrees.

Name _____

Critical Vocabulary

▶ **Read each sentence. Underline the sentence that best fits the meaning of the word in dark print.**

1. sheer

There wasn't an easy way to climb the wall, which was straight up and down.

Luckily, even though we had a long way to climb, the rocks formed stairs.

2. ascending

We braced for the airplane's bumpy landing.

The city looked smaller and smaller as the airplane climbed high up into the sky.

3. rank

What are your top five movies of all time?

I really couldn't choose which movie to watch.

4. analysis

Before my book club, I thought carefully about the book's message.

Sometimes, I like reading a book without thinking too much about its meaning.

5. variations

I'm not sure how to describe my style, as I dress a little differently every day.

Because we wore uniforms to school, we didn't have to worry about choosing a different outfit every day.

▶ **Choose one of the Critical Vocabulary words and use it in a sentence.**

_____

_____

_____

Name _____

Central Idea

The **central idea** is what the text is mostly about. Text features, such as headings, visuals, and topic sentences, often hint at the central idea. Readers evaluate supporting details to determine the central idea.

▶ **Answer the questions about pages 42–43 of *The Dawn Wall*.**

1. What is the main idea on pages 42–43?

_____

_____

2. What text evidence supports the main idea?

_____

_____

_____

▶ **Answer the questions about another page of *The Dawn Wall*.**

3. What does the photograph or infographic show?

_____

_____

4. Summarize how the photograph or infographic supports the central idea of the text, and include supporting details.

_____

_____

_____

_____

Name _____

Latin Roots tract, duc, tribut; Greek Root graph

> Work with a partner. Using your knowledge of roots, predict the meaning of each word. Then use a print or online dictionary to confirm or correct the meanings of each word.

Root	Word	Meaning
tract	traction	
duc	deduce	
tribut	contribution	
graph	choreographer	

> Write a sentence for each word in the chart.

_____
_____
_____
_____
_____
_____
_____
_____
_____
_____
_____
_____
_____
_____

Media Techniques

Media techniques present information and might include sound elements, expert speakers, live action, animation, or visual elements.

> Answer the questions about the video *Meet the Climbers Who Made Yosemite's Toughest Ascent* on page 50.

1. What does the video contribute to your understanding that the text, infographics, and photo essay alone do not provide?

_____

_____

_____

2. What media techniques are used in the video?

_____

_____

> Answer these questions about the photo essay that begins on page 44 of *The Dawn Wall.*

3. Examine the photographs on pages 44 and 45 in the photo essay. What do they add to your experience as a viewer? Explain to a partner what they help you visualize.

_____

_____

_____

4. How do the close-up photo of the climber's hand on page 46 and the accompanying text help readers better understand free climbing?

_____

_____

Name _____

Vowel Sounds /ou/, /o͞o/, /ô/, /oi/

> Read each sentence. Find the word or words with the vowel sounds /ou/, /o͞o/, /ô/, or /oi/. Underline the vowels that stand for the sound.

1. The explorers left for a long voyage across the Atlantic Ocean.

2. Can I please have a penny to toss into the fountain?

3. My favorite animal to draw is the baboon.

4. The basement was filled with sawdust after my grandfather cut the wood.

5. Can you please hand me the hammer from the toolbox?

6. Ramona wore a turquoise dress to the pool party.

7. Uncle Charles bought me a new laptop as a graduation gift.

8. The band director told me I did an outstanding job at the concert.

Name _____

Critical Vocabulary

> Complete each sentence using a Critical Vocabulary word in the Word Bank.

descent	propaganda	deport	viewpoints	phenomenon
endorsement	hurdle	dubious	indigenous	

1. The professional athlete has many _____ deals that keep her very busy.

2. A country may _____ someone who does not have legal status.

3. There are three types of plants that are _____ to our state.

4. My brother was _____ that I would actually help him with his homework.

5. Misleading information, or _____ , attempts to sway people's opinions.

6. My family is of Spanish and Irish _____ .

7. The inventor overcame one final _____ , and her invention was complete.

8. Debates are interesting because they present various _____ .

9. The baseball _____ was given a major league contract.

> Choose two of the Critical Vocabulary words and use them in a sentence.

_____

_____

Name _____

Text Structure

Text structure refers to how a text is organized. Authors may use more than one text structure within a selection. Text structure is related to the author's purpose for writing.

▶ **Answer the questions about pages 58–59 of *9 Young People Who Changed the World.***

1. What cause-and-effect text structures can you identify?

_____

_____

_____

_____

_____

2. How does cause-and-effect text structure reveal the main idea?

_____

_____

_____

▶ **Answer the questions about pages 66–67 of *9 Young People Who Changed the World.***

3. What examples of cause-and-effect text structures can you find on these pages?

_____

_____

_____

_____

_____

4. How does cause-and-effect text structure support the author's purpose?

_____

_____

_____

Name _____

Prefixes semi–, sur–

> Complete the chart by adding two words that contain the prefix *semi*– and two that contain the prefix *sur*–. Using your knowledge of these prefixes, predict the meaning of each word. Then use a print or online dictionary to confirm or correct the meaning of each word.

Word Part	Word	Meaning
semi–		
sur–		

> Write a sentence for each word in the chart.

_____

_____

_____

_____

_____

_____

_____

_____

_____

_____

_____

_____

_____

24

Name _____

Author's Purpose

Author's purpose is the reason for writing. Authors choose a text structure that helps them get their ideas across to the reader.

> **Answer the questions about page 61 of** *9 Young People Who Changed the World.*

1. What is the author's purpose?

_____

_____

2. What is the importance of this information?

_____

_____

3. Why does the author include Anne's father's reaction to the discovery of Anne's diary?

_____

_____

_____

> **Answer the question about** *9 Young People Who Changed the World.*

4. What is the author's purpose for writing about both Sophie Scholl and Anne Frank?

_____

_____

_____

_____

Vowel Sounds /ou/, /ōo/, /ô/, /oi/

▶ **Read each sentence. Find the word from the box that makes the most sense in the sentence. Make sure it has the sound noted below the blank. Then, write the word in the blank.**

/ou/ words	/ōo/ words	/ô/ words	/oi/ words
drought, discount	afternoon, mushrooms	shawl, cough	destroy, rejoiced

1. The farmer was relieved when the rainfall brought an end to the _____ .
   /ou/ sound

2. Kate wrapped a _____ across her shoulders because she was cold.
   /ô/ sound

3. Rene bought the sweater on sale at a thirty percent _____ .
   /ou/ sound

4. The _____ grew quickly in the warm, wet climate.
   /ōo/ sound

5. The children were afraid that the ocean waves would _____ their
   sand castle.
   /oi/ sound

6. We get out of school at three o'clock in the _____ .
   /ōo/ sound

7. To prevent the spread of germs, please cover your mouth when you _____ .
   /ô/sound

8. The couple _____ when they found their lost dog in the animal shelter.
   /oi/ sound

Name _____

Text and Graphic Features

In informational texts, authors use **text features** such as captions, boldface words, and headings to relay information clearly. **Graphic features** such as maps, photos, and charts further explain or reinforce ideas in the main text.

▶ **Answer the questions about page 67 of *9 Young People Who Changed the World*.**

1. What information does the map provide for readers?

_____

_____

_____

_____

2. If this text did not include a map, what other text or graphic features could give readers a sense of location?

_____

_____

_____

▶ **Answer the questions about *9 Young People Who Changed the World*.**

3. Why does the author include the introduction on page 55?

_____

_____

_____

4. How does the diagram of the braille system on page 59 support the main text?

_____

_____

_____

Vowel + /r/ Sounds

> Read each sentence. Find the word or words in the sentence with a vowel + /r/ sound. Underline the letters that stand for the *r*-controlled sound.

1. What projects are you doing in art class?

2. State officials voted to change the unfair law.

3. I hope we see some reindeer grazing when we visit the Alaskan frontier.

4. My aunt is an artist who creates cartoons.

5. Those pearls go perfectly with that dress.

6. Anabelle plans to attend many movie premiers this year.

7. I forgot to take my new band uniform to the game.

8. I can't believe this shirt has fur on it.

Critical Vocabulary

You can use the words you learn from reading as you talk and write.

> **Use details from *Identity Theft* to complete the sentence stems below. Be sure to demonstrate the meaning of each Critical Vocabulary word.**

1. A successful **imitation** diamond should

_____

_____ .

2. His mother showed her **indifference** to what was going on with the other adults by

_____

_____ .

3. Good friends might act **spitefully** toward each other if

_____

_____ .

4. A decision is reached after a jury has **pondered**

_____

_____ .

5. After getting an ice cream cone, the little girl **fumed** when

_____

_____ .

6. After my grandmother knew she could trust me, she **confided** that

_____

_____ .

Name _____

7. When they were **escorting** the wild horses to a new pasture, the cowboys

_____

_____ .

8. The raccoons come to the campsite and **habitually**

_____

_____ .

9. Judging from the footprints in the wet cement, the workmen **surmised** that

_____

_____ .

> **Choose two of the Critical Vocabulary words and use them in a sentence.**

_____ .

_____ .

Name _____

Literary Elements

Literary elements are the pieces that make up a story. They include the **characters**, or animals and people in the story. Another literary element is the **setting**, or where and when the story takes place. The **plot** and events that take place in the story are also literary elements.

▶ **Answer the questions about paragraphs 6–11 of** *Identity Theft.*

1. Describe the original Ana's behavior as shown in paragraphs 6–11.

_____

_____

_____

_____

2. How does Ana's behavior affect the plot?

_____

_____

_____

_____

▶ **Answer these questions about a cause-and-effect event from** *Identity Theft.*

3. What is the cause and effect, and what transitional words signal this organization?

_____

_____

4. How does this event affect the plot of the story?

_____

_____

Name _____

Vowel + /r/ Sounds

> Read each sentence. Find a word from the chart that best completes the sentence.
Write the word on the line and underline the vowel + /r/ sound. Not every word will be used.

/är/ words	garnish, pharmacy
/âr/ words	impair, transparent, solitaire
/ôr/ words	explore, adorable, afford, torn
/ûr/ words	virtually, nurse, circulation
/îr/ words	pioneer, sightseer, dreary

1. Cities like Rome, London, and New York offer many activities for a _____ .

2. A plate of food in a restaurant often has a parsley sprig used as a _____ .

3. The _____ panda cubs posed for their first appearance in public.

4. I can see through the curtains because they are made of _____ cloth.

5. We saved our money so that we could _____ to buy a special gift for our grandparents.

6. I am amazed that _____ all vegetables contain fructose or simple sugar.

7. Rob picked up his prescription at the _____ .

8. When it's foggy and _____ outside, I like to play board games inside.

9. The doctor told me that loud noises might _____ my hearing.

10. Good blood _____ is important for good health.

Name _____

Root gen; Prefix en–; Suffixes –y, –ly, –ily

The prefix **en–** (meaning "within, in") is found in words such as **enable** and **enlighten**. The root **gen** (meaning "something produced or created") is found in words such as **gender** and **gene**. The suffixes **–y**, **–ly**, and **–ily** (meaning "like," "characterized by," or "inclined to") are found in words such as **creamy** and **greasy**, as well as **lazily** and **angrily**, or **smoothly** and **sadly**.

▶ Complete the chart with other words that contain the root **gen** and the prefix **en–** and the suffixes **–y**, **–ly**, and **–ily**.

gen	en–	–y, –ly, –ily
_____	_____	_____
_____	_____	_____
_____	_____	_____
_____	_____	_____
_____	_____	_____

▶ Write a sentence for each word in the chart.

_____

_____

_____

_____

_____

_____

_____

_____

_____

Name _____

Theme

The **theme** of a story is the main message, moral, or lesson of the text. The theme is often implied, or not directly stated. You can use text clues within the events, the character's behavior, or other details to discover the theme.

▶ **Answer the questions about paragraphs 1–23 of *Identity Theft*.**

1. What is the author's message or theme?

_____

_____

_____

_____

2. How is the theme related to the title?

_____

_____

_____

_____

▶ **A story may have more than one theme. Answer the questions about another event from *Identity Theft*.**

3. How does original Ana react to the event?

_____

_____

4. How does original Ana's reaction to the event help you figure out the theme?

_____

_____

Name _____

Point of View

All stories are told from a narrator's **point of view.**

> **Answer the questions about page 86 of *Identity Theft.***

1. How can you tell *Identity Theft* is told from the third-person point of view?

_____

_____

_____

_____

2. What type of third-person point of view does the author use?

_____

_____

_____

_____

> **Answer the questions about a character other than original Ana from *Identity Theft.***

3. How would the story be different if it was told from this character's point of view?

_____

_____

_____

4. What would this character think about the events of the story? Choose an event from the story and write this character's thoughts and feelings about it.

_____

_____

_____

Words with *ie* or *ei*

> Read each sentence. Write the letters *ie* or *ei* in the blank space to complete the word.

1. Last Sunday, we played softball in the new f____ld.

2. The police officer caught the th____f before he could escape.

3. My grandmother likes to swim laps in the pool during her l____sure time.

4. The h____ght of the new building downtown is 200 meters.

5. The clerk was angry when he found a counterf____t coin in the register.

6. Do you think you're strong enough to lift that heavy w____ght?

7. My aunt is still gr____ving over the loss of her beloved pet.

8. One of my favorite hobbies is reading about anc____nt cultures.

Name _____

Critical Vocabulary

> Read each sentence. Underline the sentence that best fits the meaning of the word in dark print.

1. slackening

It had been storming all day, but the rain finally started slowing down.

The wind blew faster and faster as the day went on.

2. frail

Though she fell out of the tree, she jumped up and kept playing as if nothing had happened.

I've mostly recovered from the accident, but the leg that I broke is still a little weak.

3. drenched

Wring out that dripping sponge before you use it.

After the desert hike, I was incredibly thirsty for water.

4. savagely

Wanting to make a good impression, I carefully cut my food and used good table manners.

I was so hungry that I didn't care how I looked as I tore into the sandwich.

5. resilient

The hurricane battered the town, but its people worked together to rebuild quickly.

Even though the houses were well-built, the tornado still knocked them all down.

> Choose one of the Critical Vocabulary words and use it in a sentence.

_____

_____

Name _____

Theme

The **theme** of a story is its message, lesson, or moral. A theme can be clearly stated, such as at the end of a fable. It can also be implied, or hinted at, through the story's characters, settings, and events.

▶ **Answer the questions about paragraphs 53–54 of** *All Summer in a Day.*

1. When the teacher warns the students not to go too far, the students do not listen. What do they do instead?

   _____

   _____

   _____

2. How does the theme "think before you act" relate to these paragraphs? How does it connect to what the students did to Margot?

   _____

   _____

   _____

▶ **Answer these additional questions about theme in** *All Summer in a Day.*

3. Why are the students slow to let Margot out of the closet?

   _____

   _____

   _____

4. What do you think the students learned from their actions?

   _____

   _____

   _____

Words with *ie* or *ei*

▶ **Read each sentence. Choose the word that is spelled correctly and write it on the line.**

1. They say appearances can be _____ , so you should not judge a book by
   its cover.   (deceiving, decieving)

2. Katie wants to paint the _____ walls in her room a bright orange.
                             (biege, beige)

3. I wonder what kind of _____ our puppy will get into today.
                          (mischief, mischeif)

4. Researchers discovered a new _____ of frogs in the rainforest.
                                (species, speceis)

5. When the plane took off, a baby let out a _____ cry.
                                          (peircing, piercing)

6. Don't put off your dreams; _____ the day!
                             (seize, sieze)

7. The golden _____ is one of the most popular dogs in the United States.
             (retreiver, retriever)

8. We learned that _____ keep blood flowing to the heart.
                   (viens, veins)

Name _____

Critical Vocabulary

> **Answer the questions below.**

1. About how far back in time would you need to travel to visit the **Victorian** era?

   _____

   _____ .

2. If you walked into a room with a gloomy **atmosphere**, what might you assume?

   _____

   _____ .

3. What makes voting in the United States **democratic**?

   _____

   _____ .

4. What in your life has **transformed** you the most?

   _____

   _____ .

5. What activities do you **associate** with the end-of-year holidays?

   _____

   _____

> **Choose one of the Critical Vocabulary words and use it in a sentence.**

   _____

   _____

   _____

   _____

Name _____

Figurative Language

Sometimes authors use literal language, which means that the words in the text have the same meaning that they have in a dictionary. Sometimes they use **figurative language** instead, in which words mean something different from their dictionary definitions.

> **Answer the questions about paragraph 9 of** *It's More Than Just Rain or Snow or Springtime.*

1. What type of figurative language does the author use when describing Noah and the flood?

_____

_____

2. What does this metaphor mean?

_____

_____

> **Answer the questions about pages 111–112 of** *It's More Than Just Rain or Snow or Springtime.*

3. According to the author of the text, what are some figurative meanings of fog in a text?

_____

_____

4. What type of weather can be "threatening, inviting, playful, [or] suffocating," according to the author of the text? Why?

_____

_____

Name _____

Latin Root ject; Prefixes trans-, inter-

> Work with a partner. Using your knowledge of prefixes and roots, predict the meaning of each word. Then use a print or online dictionary to confirm or correct the meanings of each word.

Root or Prefix	Word	Meaning
ject	trajectory	
trans–	translate	
inter–	intermission	
ject, inter–	interject	

> Write a sentence for each word in the chart.

_____

_____

_____

_____

_____

_____

_____

_____

_____

_____

_____

_____

Name _____

Ideas and Support

Most nonfiction text uses a system of **ideas and support**, in which the author makes a **claim** (the central or main idea) and then supports that claim with **evidence** from the text, from real life, or from elsewhere. Readers can identify the main ideas in a text and then find the facts that support the main ideas.

▷ **Answer the questions about paragraphs 5–7 of** *It's More Than Just Rain or Snow or Springtime.*

1. What is the main idea?

_____

_____

2. What claim is the author making about the main idea?

_____

_____

3. What details support the author's claim?

_____

_____

_____

▷ **Answer the questions about paragraphs 19–20 of** *It's More Than Just Rain or Snow or Springtime.*

4. In paragraphs 19 and 20, how would you explain the author's purpose or message?

_____

_____

5. Is the message fact or opinion? Explain.

_____

_____

Name _____

6. Who do you think is the author's intended audience for his ideas about the seasons and literature?

_____

_____

_____

▶ **Answer the questions about page 114 of** *It's More Than Just Rain or Snow or Springtime.*

7. What conclusion can you draw about the author's main idea in paragraph 21, beginning "Or take Henry James"?

_____

_____

8. What details does the author use to support the main idea you identified?

_____

_____

Name _____

Words with /ən/, /əl/, /ər/

▶ Choose a word from the Word Bank with the /ən/, /əl/, and /ər/ schwa sound to complete each sentence. Write the word on the blank. Not all of the words have the schwa sound.

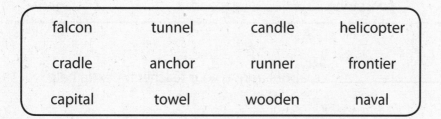

falcon	tunnel	candle	helicopter
cradle	anchor	runner	frontier
capital	towel	wooden	naval

1. Be sure to have a _____ ready in case the power goes out.

2. Can you please take the _____ blocks out of the toy chest?

3. We watched the _____ catch its prey using its feet.

4. Drop the _____ as soon as the ship reaches the port.

5. Harold was relieved when he saw the rescue _____ appear in the distance.

6. Columbus is the _____ of Ohio.

7. The crowd cheered as the last _____ crossed the finish line.

8. Please use a paper _____ to clean up the spill.

Name _____

Critical Vocabulary

> Complete each sentence using a Critical Vocabulary word in the Word Bank.

overcome	fleeting	miserable	demeaning
elope	conspiring	garland	outraged

1. There is nothing _____ about asking your teacher for extra help.

2. Just before going on stage, the actor was suddenly _____ with fear.

3. In some cultures, the bride and groom each wear a _____ of flowers at their wedding ceremony.

4. The movie stars decided to _____ because they wanted a quiet wedding.

5. Last night, I caught a _____ glimpse of a falling star.

6. The football coach was _____ by the referee's decision.

7. My stuffy nose and sore throat made me feel _____ .

8. The men were arrested for _____ to overthrow the king.

> Choose two of the Critical Vocabulary words and use them in a sentence.

_____

_____

Name _____

Elements of Drama

Dramatic elements include how the drama is organized through **acts** and **scenes**. They include **dialogue** and **character tags** to let the reader know who is speaking. **Stage directions** give details about **setting**, or where the story takes place, and how the **characters** feel and act. Characters are also revealed through what they say and how they respond to other characters. A **narrator** fills in details about what's happening in the play.

> **Answer the questions about pages 120–121 of *Upside-Down and Backward*.**

1. What information do the cast of characters, prologue, and character tags provide?

   _____

   _____

   _____

2. What is the purpose of the text within parentheses in the middle of Lysander's speech in paragraph 8?

   _____

   _____

> **Answer the questions about dramatic elements in *Upside-Down and Backward*.**

3. What does Helena's dialogue in paragraph 16 reveal to the reader?

   _____

   _____

   _____

   _____

4. Using paragraph 32, describe Puck's role and contribution to the drama.

   _____

   _____

   _____

Name _____

Suffixes –ful, –less, –ment, –ness

> Combine each of the following words with one or more of the suffixes. Use a dictionary to help you figure out which suffixes can be used for each word. Write down the meaning of each new word you create and its part of speech.

1. hope

_____

_____

_____

2. pay

_____

_____

_____

3. clever

_____

_____

_____

4. motion

_____

_____

_____

> Look at each new word and its meaning. Write a sentence with each new word.

_____

_____

_____

Name _____

Literary Elements

Literary elements are the pieces that make up a story. **Characters** are the people and animals in a story and **setting** is where the story takes place. Characters undergo changes as they interact with other characters and with story events. The story includes a **conflict**, which is the problem that the characters face, and a **resolution**, which is how the conflict is solved.

▸ **Answer the questions about page 125 of** *Upside-Down and Backward.*

1. How does the setting of the forest in paragraph 58 contribute to the story?

_____

_____

_____

2. How does Puck contribute to the conflict?

_____

_____

_____

▸ **Answer the questions about page 126 of** *Upside-Down and Backward.*

3. In paragraph 65, find and interpret the meaning of an idiom.

_____

_____

_____

4. How can you use context to figure out the meaning of this idiom?

_____

_____

_____

Name _____

5. Why do you suppose the author uses the word *clueless* instead of *unaware*?

_____

_____

_____

▶ **Answer the questions about the characters in *Upside-Down and Backward*.**

6. At the end of Scene 1 on page 123, why does Helena decide not to keep Hermia's secret?

_____

_____

_____

_____

7. In Scene 4, why do Helena and Hermia become angry with each other?

_____

_____

_____

Name _____

Words with /ən/, /əl/, /ər/

> Read each sentence. Find the word from the Word Bank with the schwa sound that makes the most sense in the sentence. Then, write the word in the blank.

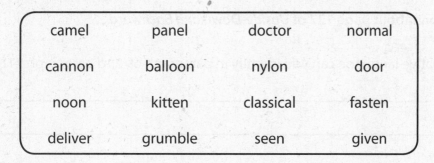

camel	panel	doctor	normal
cannon	balloon	nylon	door
noon	kitten	classical	fasten
deliver	grumble	seen	given

1. The post office will _____ my package by the end of the week.

2. The soldiers wheeled the large _____ down the hill.

3. Sammy smiled as the _____ purred softly on his lap.

4. My brother and I saw a _____ at the zoo.

5. I heard my brother _____ under his breath after he lost the game.

6. My father enjoys listening to _____ music while he washes dishes.

7. My mother visited the _____ after her car accident.

8. Make sure to _____ your seat belt before the drive home.

Name _____

Figurative Language

Authors often use **figurative language** for a special effect or feeling or to make a point about the characters, setting, or plot.

> **Answer the questions about page 127 of *Upside-Down and Backward*.**

1. What types of figurative language can you identify in paragraph 69 and paragraph 71?

_____

_____

2. How would you explain the meaning of each?

_____

_____

_____

_____

> **Answer the questions about figurative language in *Upside-Down and Backward*.**

3. In paragraph 16, Helena says to Hermia "you, with your starry eyes and your sweet voice. I wish some of your beauty would rub off on me." Identify and explain the meaning of the figures of speech.

_____

_____

_____

_____

_____

_____

Name _____

4. In paragraph 30, Helena says of Demetrius: "But then, he decided he wanted her and his promises to me melted like snow in the hot sun." Identify and explain the figure of speech.

_____

_____

_____

_____

5. How does figurative language contribute to the meaning of the text?

_____

_____

_____

_____

Name _____

Commonly Confused Words

▷ **Choose the correct word within the parentheses to complete each sentence. Write the word on the line.**

1. Make sure you pack warm-weather (clothes, cloths) _____ for the trip to the beach.

2. During allergy season and when I have a cold, it is difficult to (breath, breathe) _____ through my nose.

3. My friend Alicia has such a cheerful, (hardy, hearty) _____ laugh.

4. The teacher (choose, chose) _____ me to help hand out the papers.

5. All the dogs jumped in the lake (except, accept) _____ my dog, Rufus, who is afraid of water.

6. Did you know the new restaurant in town was (formally, formerly) _____ an old cotton mill?

7. Since the weather is warming up, I'm not (averse, adverse) _____ to having a picnic outdoors.

8. Jack usually chooses apple pie for (desert, dessert) _____ .

9. Can you (advice, advise) _____ us on which way to go?

10. Turn left and then (proceed, precede) _____ to the next light.

Critical Vocabulary

You can use the words you learn from reading as you talk and write.

> **Use details from the selection to complete the sentence stems below. Be sure to demonstrate the meaning of each Critical Vocabulary word.**

1. After the wind blew the papers **haphazardly** across the lawn, we

   _____.

2. Our cat was **captivated** by a ball of yarn on the floor and

   _____.

3. The smell of the casserole was very **appealing**, but its taste

   _____.

4. The silverware was arranged in an **orderly** manner so that

   _____.

5. The reporters **bombarded** the star of the game with so many questions that

   _____.

6. After watching a movie about a famous inventor, my brain was **stimulated** with

   _____.

7. At first the robot could only make **crude** drawings, but soon

   _____.

8. The police investigators will eventually **dissect** the events of the crime and

   _____.

Name _____

9. If your handwriting lacks **precision**, you need to

_____ .

10. The invention of the cell phone was viewed as **revolutionary** because

_____ .

> **Choose two of the Critical Vocabulary words and use them in a sentence.**

_____

_____

Name _____

Text Structure

Authors of narrative nonfiction texts use **text structure** to help readers understand and recognize how ideas are connected. **Sequence** puts events in the order in which they happened. Transition words such as *first, second, next, finally*, and *after* show sequence.

> **Answer the questions about page 153 of *The Boy Who Invented TV*.**

1. In paragraphs 7–9, locate transition words or phrases that help sequence events.

_____

_____

2. Reword paragraphs 8 and 9, using alternative transition words and phrases to keep events in sequential order.

_____

_____

_____

> **Answer these additional questions about *The Boy Who Invented TV*.**

3. Why do you think the author describes events from Philo's childhood before telling about his invention of TV?

_____

_____

_____

4. Why do you think the author uses the text structure of sequence to tell about Philo's life?

_____

_____

_____

Decoding

Name _____

Commonly Confused Words

> Read the words in the Word Bank. Choose the correct word to complete each sentence. Write the word on the line provided.

human	farther	respectfully	since	appraise
humane	further	respectively	sense	apprise

1. Is NASA working on sending a _____ to Mars?

2. Ms. Parker will _____ the house so we know what it's worth.

3. Vince has such a good _____ of humor.

4. The mountain is _____ away than it looks.

5. Many farmers practice _____ farming, allowing their animals to roam freely.

6. Abby, Naomi, and Brooke play soccer, volleyball, and baseball _____ .

7. The scientists do not have conclusive results, so they need _____ research.

8. After we finish our research, we will _____ the group of what we learned.

9. I _____ declined the invitation to the party.

10. _____ you arrived early, you can help me set the table.

Name _____

Prefix tele-; Greek Roots electr, electro, phon

The prefix **tele–** (meaning "far off") is found in words such as **telegram** and **telephone**.
You can find the Greek roots **electr** and **electro** (meaning "amber" or "charged with power")
in words such as **electrical** and **electromagnet**. The Greek root **phon** (meaning "sound") is
found in words such as **telephone** and **phonics**.

▶ **Complete the chart with other words that contain the prefix** tele– **and the Greek roots**
electro **and** phon.

tele–	electr, electro	phon
_____	_____	_____
_____	_____	_____
_____	_____	_____
_____	_____	_____
_____	_____	_____
_____		

▶ **Write a sentence for each word in the chart.**

_____

_____

_____

_____

_____

_____

_____

Name _____

Literary Elements

Literary elements are the pieces that make up a narrative. They include **characters**, or the people and animals in a narrative, and **setting**, or where and when a narrative takes place. Setting can influence the decisions that characters make, and characters' decisions can influence the plot.

> **Answer the questions about pages 156–157 of *The Boy Who Invented TV.***

1. List details about the Snake River Valley setting that may have influenced Philo to become an inventor.

   _____

   _____

   _____

2. How is Philo's inventive curiosity revealed through his actions?

   _____

   _____

   _____

   _____

> **Answer these questions about page 159 of *The Boy Who Invented TV.***

3. What does Philo compare electricity to in paragraph 36?

   _____

   _____

4. What does this comparison help you understand about electrons?

   _____

   _____

5. Philo wanted to "harness" electrons. What is another word with a similar denotation as *harness*?

   _____

   _____

Name _____

> **Answer these additional questions about** *The Boy Who Invented TV.*

6. What does the relationship between Philo and his wife Pem tell you about Pem?

    _____

    _____

7. How do you think the plot focusing on Philo's life would have been different without Pem?

    _____

    _____

Name _____

Author's Purpose

An **author's purpose** is the reason for writing. Some authors write to **persuade**, or get readers to think or act in a certain way. Others write to **inform**, or share, information about a topic. Still others write to **entertain**, or amuse, readers. Text structure and other techniques help authors achieve their purpose.

▶ **Answer the questions about page 159 of** *The Boy Who Invented TV.*

1. Is the purpose of these paragraphs to persuade, inform, or entertain? What effect does that have on readers?

_____

_____

2. How does the author use cause and effect in these paragraphs?

_____

_____

3. What can you infer from the information gathered?

_____

_____

▶ **Answer additional questions about page 159 of** *The Boy Who Invented TV.*

4. What word in paragraph 36 signals a cause-and-effect text structure?

_____

_____

5. How does the cause-and-effect text structure on this page help achieve the author's purpose?

_____

_____

Name _____

VV Syllable Division Pattern

> The words in the Word Bank all have the VV syllable division pattern. Write a word from the box that best completes each sentence. Then, draw a line to separate the two syllables in each word.

chaos	react	poem	giant
triumph	diem	trial	fluent

1. The judge and jury sat patiently during the lengthy _____ .

2. Gary felt a sense of _____ after winning the championship.

3. Sara wrote the most beautiful _____ in class today.

4. The basement was in total _____ after my parents left the room.

5. My sister is _____ in three languages.

6. Carpe _____ means "seize the day in Latin."

7. The _____ panda ate bamboo throughout the day.

8. How would you _____ if you won the school talent contest?

Name _____

Critical Vocabulary

> Read each sentence. Underline the sentence that best fits the meaning of the word in dark print.

1. cipher

The agent compared the message to the code to determine the letters.

The agent hid the message at the bottom of her bag and hoped that nobody would find it.

2. sophisticated

The old cell phone was pretty simple, as all you could use it for was making and receiving calls.

Newer cell phones do many complicated tasks, such as taking photos and searching the Internet.

3. theory

The mathematician based her ideas on the rules she had been taught about negative numbers.

The math team was unsure about their answer, so they double-checked their work.

4. miscellaneous

Before I started, I carefully laid out all the ingredients I would need to bake the cake.

After I had sorted the building supplies, I had a few leftover nails that didn't belong anywhere.

5. pursuers

We ducked down an alley to hide from the kids who were following us.

We enjoyed a quiet stroll down the empty street.

> **Choose one of the Critical Vocabulary words and use it in a sentence.**

_____

_____

_____

_____

Name _____

Literary Elements

Literary elements are the pieces that make up a story—characters, setting, plot, conflict, and resolution. You need to be able to identify the literary elements in a story in order to understand them.

> **Answer the questions about page 170 of** *The Secret Science Alliance and the Copycat Crook.*

1. What secret is Julian hiding and why?

_____

_____

2. At the beginning of the story, what problem is Julian trying to solve?

_____

_____

> **Answer these questions about pages 173–175 of** *The Secret Science Alliance and the Copycat Crook.*

3. How does the author build up suspense in advance of the conflict?

_____

_____

_____

4. What predictions can you make about the plot based on this?

_____

_____

_____

Name _____

> **Answer these questions about *The Secret Science Alliance and the Copycat Crook*.**

5. Why do Ben and Greta play a word association game with Julian?

_____

_____

_____

_____

6. How does the meeting with Ben and Greta change Julian?

_____

_____

_____

_____

VV Syllable Division Pattern

> For each sentence below, find a word in the Word Bank that has the VV syllable division pattern with each vowel making its own sound. Write it on the line. Then draw a line to separate the syllables. Not every word has the VV syllable division pattern.

preorder	season	dial	people
trio	bias	author	meow
tourist	diet	create	fluid

1. My mom, dad, and I sang in a _____ at the concert.

2. The magazine writer knows that she cannot show any _____ in her articles.

3. Our pet bird needs to be on a special _____ .

4. My uncle forgot to put wiper _____ in his car so he couldn't clean his windshield.

5. Maybe I didn't _____ the right number.

6. When our cat is hungry or lonely, she will _____ loudly.

7. Sometimes we _____ our food at the restaurant so we don't have to wait.

8. The art teacher asked his students to _____ a sculpture out of clay.

Name _____

Critical Vocabulary

> Read each sentence. Underline the sentence that best fits the meaning of the word in dark print.

1. households

I live with my parents and my grandmother.
My house has two bedrooms and one bathroom, along with an attic.

2. livestock

I helped out in the vegetable garden, pulling weeds and watering the tomatoes.
The cows were uneasy during the storm, so the farmer stayed with them.

> Choose one of the Critical Vocabulary words and use it in a sentence.

_____

_____

_____

_____

_____

_____

_____

_____

_____

_____

_____

_____

_____

Name _____

Text Structure

Text structure is the way an author organizes a text. Recognizing a text's structure can help readers connect the author's ideas to events in the text.

> **Answer the questions about paragraphs 4–6 of *Lions No Match for a Young Boy and His Invention*.**

1. How does the author organize ideas in this part of the text?

_____

2. What examples of this text structure can you identify?

_____

_____

_____

> **Answer the question about the video *Lion Lights*.**

3. Identify a cause-and-effect text structure from the video.

_____

_____

> **Answer the questions about text structure in *Lions No Match for a Young Boy and His Invention*.**

4. What cause-and-effect text structure can you identify?

_____

5. How does the text structure connect ideas and help readers understand the text?

_____

_____

Name _____

Latin Roots *sol, rad*; Greek Root *aero*

> Work with a partner. Using your knowledge of the roots, predict the meaning of each word. Then use a print or online dictionary to confirm or correct the meanings of each word.

Root	Word	Meaning
aero	aerobic	
sol	parasol	
rad	radiate	

> Write a sentence for each word in the chart.

_____

_____

_____

_____

_____

_____

_____

_____

_____

_____

_____

_____

_____

_____

Media Techniques

Media techniques are tools that help communicate ideas and meaning to audiences. These tools can include visual and sound elements. Media techniques help viewers better understand a topic and how ideas are related.

▷ **Answer the questions about the video *Lion Lights.***

1. How are media techniques used effectively in *Lion Lights*?

_____

_____

_____

_____

2. How is the overall message of the video effective?

_____

_____

_____

▷ **Answer the questions about *Lions No Match for Young Boy and His Invention.***

3. How do the photos in the article add to your understanding of the video?

_____

_____

_____

4. How do the text and video work together to help you understand Turere's problem and solution?

_____

_____

_____

Words with Final /īz/, /ĭv/, /ĭj/

> Read each sentence. Circle the word with final /īz/, /ĭv/, or /ĭj/ that makes sense in the sentence.

1. This machine can _____ rock into tiny pieces.

   pulverize   magnetize

2. The doctor wrapped a _____ around the patient's cut.

   package   bandage

3. Alice is very _____ of her little brother.

   assertive   protective

4. When no one answers the door, Kate will _____ there is something wrong.

   surprise   surmise

5. The bully was punished for being too _____ on the playground.

   aggressive   manipulative

6. The magician will _____ everyone with an amazing trick.

   advertise   surprise

7. My eyes were _____ to the light after watching the movie in the dark.

   sensitive   abrasive

8. Please leave me a _____ if I am not home to receive your call.

   beverage   message

9. John received a large _____ from his grandparents.

   signage   package

10. You will need to _____ to the principal for being rude.

    apologize   mesmerize

Name _____

Critical Vocabulary

▶ **Complete each sentence using a Critical Vocabulary word in the Word Bank.**

sterile	artery	abdomen	efficacy	replicate
integrated	amateur	prosthetics	liable	

1. The teacher explained that a/an _____ is one of many blood vessels that carry blood away from the heart.

2. My uncle is a/an _____ chef who loves making great meals for his family.

3. The operating room had to be thoroughly cleaned to make sure it was _____ .

4. My neighbor is _____ for the damage his dog did to my garden.

5. The _____ contains many important organs, including the gall bladder and liver.

6. A new library has been _____ into our county library system.

7. Is there information on the _____ of chicken soup for the common cold?

8. The company specializes in making _____ for soldiers who have been wounded in war.

9. We enjoyed the meal at the restaurant and hoped to _____ it at home.

▶ **Choose two of the Critical Vocabulary words and use each word in a different sentence.**

_____

_____

Name _____

Text Structure

Authors of informational texts may use **text structure** to present information in **logical order** to readers. Transitional words help readers identify the text structure being used.

> **Answer the questions about page 200 of** *3D Printing: Imagination in Technology.*

1. What text structure can you identify in paragraphs 7–9?

_____

_____

2. What transitional words or phrases signal this structure?

_____

_____

3. Explain how the text structure contributes to the author's purpose.

_____

_____

_____

> **Answer the questions about paragraphs 12–15 of** *3D Printing: Imagination in Technology.*

4. What text structure does the author use in the section "How 3D Printing Works"?

_____

_____

5. Why do you think the author uses this structure?

_____

_____

_____

Name _____

Prefixes com-, con-

> Complete the chart by adding two other words that contain the prefix *com–* and two that contain the prefix *con–*. Using your knowledge of these prefixes, predict the meaning of each word. Then use a print or online dictionary to confirm or correct the meaning of each word.

Word Part	Word	Meaning
com–	complete	
	community	
con–	confer	
	conduct	

> Write a sentence for each word in the chart.

_____

_____

_____

_____

_____

_____

_____

_____

_____

_____

_____

_____

Name _____

Author's Purpose

An **author's purpose** in an informational text is to inform readers about a topic. Sometimes, authors can also include other purposes, such as to persuade the reader that something is true or that they should do something.

▶ **Answer the questions about the section "How 3D Printing Works" of** *3D Printing: Imagination in Technology.*

1. What is the author's purpose in this section?

_____

_____

2. What does the author say is the effect of CAD software?

_____

_____

3. How does the author's point of view contribute to the purpose for writing?

_____

_____

_____

▶ **Answer the questions about** *3D Printing: Imagination in Technology.*

4. Why does the author include information about food, manufacturing, and prosthetics?

_____

_____

5. What can you infer about the author's desire to share this information?

_____

_____

_____

Words with Final /īz/, /ĭv/, /ĭj/

▶ In each sentence, there is a word that needs an ending. Choose an ending from the box that will complete the word and make sense in the sentence.

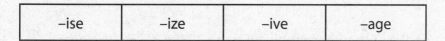

–ise	–ize	–ive	–age

1. Amanda ran out of the room when she saw the repuls_____ bug.

2. Martha returned the toaster because it was defect_____ .

3. The aver_____ test score in Mr. Plummer's class was 85.

4. Who would like to summar_____ what has happened in the story so far?

5. Dylan winced when the dentist touched his sensit_____ tooth.

6. Storing the chemicals properly will minim_____ the danger of an accident.

7. The home team had the advant_____ in the baseball game.

8. The director will superv_____ a large staff at the studio.

Name _____

Text and Graphic Features

Authors of informational texts often include **text features** (such as bold text, headings, and sidebars) and **graphic features** (such as diagrams and photographs) to explain or elaborate on the information in the text.

> **Answer the questions about the infographic on page 203 of *3D Technology: Imagination in Technology*.**

1. What does the infographic explain?

_____

2. How does the infographic help you better understand the information in "How 3D Printing Works"?

_____

_____

_____

_____

> **Answer these questions about text and graphic features in *3D Printing: Imagination in Technology*.**

3. How do text features help you understand the selection?

_____

_____

4. How do the subheadings on page 205 and bold run-in headings on page 209 help your understanding?

_____

_____

_____

Name _____

Recognize Base Words

▶ Read each sentence and underline the derivative that is formed by adding –*ion* to the base word. Then write the base word on the line provided.

1. Mr. Ruiz spends his days working on a new invention. _____

2. Earth's rotation on its axis takes twenty-four hours. _____

3. My sister's reaction to my speech was positive. _____

4. It takes years of dedication and study to become a doctor. _____

5. Will the graduation be held in the school auditorium? _____

6. Our class started a food donation drive to support the local food bank. _____

7. How many cats and dogs are available for adoption? _____

8. Cell phones are a distraction while doing homework. _____

9. Annie made a suggestion for our lunch menu. _____

10. The average elevation in our county is 2,000 feet. _____

Name _____

Critical Vocabulary

You can use the words you learn from reading as you talk and write.

> **Use details from *The Wanderer* to answer the questions below. Then use Critical Vocabulary words as you talk with a partner about your answers.**

1. What could happen if two **impulsive** people go on the same boat trip?

_____.

2. What makes *The Wanderer*'s passengers a **motley** group?

_____.

3. Sophie's mother **frets** that Sophie's cousin Cody will be on the trip. Why?

_____.

4. Why did Sophie spout a **slew** of sailing and weather terms to her family?

_____.

5. What is one of the **extensive** safety measures aboard *The Wanderer*?

_____.

6. Where did *The Wanderer* go on its **trial** run?

_____.

7. Why would plants growing along a rocky coastline be **scraggly**?

_____.

8. Why does juggling take **coordination**?

_____.

9. Why does Sophie say duty watches are **warping** her sense of time?

_____.

> **Choose two Critical Vocabulary words and use them in the same sentence.**

_____

Name _____

Literary Elements

Literary elements are the pieces that make up a story, such as **characters**, **setting**, **plot**, and **events**. Characters and setting influence what happens in a story, including the story's **conflict** and its **resolution**.

> **Answer the questions about paragraphs 97–101 of *The Wanderer*.**

1. Briefly summarize the Bompie story that Sophie tells the crew.

_____

_____

_____

2. Why do you think Sophie chose to tell this Bompie story?

_____

_____

_____

> **Answer the questions about paragraphs 70–73 of *The Wanderer*.**

3. How does Sophie describe the setting in these paragraphs?

_____

_____

_____

4. What effects do the duty watches have on Sophie?

_____

_____

_____

Name _____

> **Answer the questions about paragraphs 75–82 of *The Wanderer*.**

5. How does the setting change in this section?

_____

_____

6. How does this change in setting affect the characters?

_____

_____

> **Answer these questions about *The Wanderer*.**

7. In paragraph 10, what word in the text does the context clue *satellite navigator* help you understand? Explain.

_____

_____

8. In paragraph 85, what is another word with a similar connotation as *darlings*?

_____

_____

Recognize Base Words

> For each sentence, use the base word at the end of the sentence and write its derivative by adding –*ion*.

1. The lawyer raised an _____ during the trial. (object)

2. What _____ is Aunt Beatriz to you? (relate)

3. The school's _____ approved the new bus route. (administrate)

4. Your facial _____ suggests that you are confused. (express)

5. We read an article that describes how viral _____ spread. (infect)

6. Why do people wear hard hats at _____ sites? (construct)

7. I need help solving this mathematical _____ . (equate)

8. The roller coaster is the main _____ at the amusement park. (attract)

9. My mom talks about the many changes in technology from her _____ to mine. (generate)

10. The judge gave the first-time offender a year of _____ . (probate)

Name _____

Suffixes -al, -ic

The suffix *-al*, which means "like or related to," is found in words such as *natural* and *functional*. The suffix *-ic*, which also means "like or related to," is found in words such as *acidic* and *robotic*.

> Complete the chart with other words that contain the suffixes *-al* and *-ic*.

-al
_____
_____
_____
_____

-ic
_____
_____
_____
_____

> Write a sentence for each word in the chart.

_____

_____

_____

_____

Name _____

Figurative Language

Figurative language is words and expressions that mean something different from their dictionary definition. Figurative language creates a special effect, a feeling, or makes a point.

> Answer the questions about paragraphs 2–5 of *The Wanderer.*

1. Sophie's father calls her "Three-sided Sophie." Identify examples of figurative language and what each means.

   _____

   _____

2. What similar figurative language could describe Sophie?

   _____

   _____

> Answer the questions about paragraph 74 of *The Wanderer.*

3. Identify personification in paragraph 74.

   _____

   _____

4. What does this mean?

   _____

   _____

> Answer the question about paragraph 11 of *The Wanderer.*

5. Sophie describes Bompie as having a honey tongue. What is the purpose of this imagery?

   _____

   _____

Name _____

Point of View

Point of view refers to who is telling the story. Narrators who are part of the story use **first-person** point of view. Narrators outside of the story use **third-person** point of view. Sometimes stories are told from multiple points of view.

> **Answer the questions about the first two chapters of *The Wanderer*.**

1. From what point of view is the story told in the first two chapters? How can you tell?

   _____

   _____

   _____

2. Why do you think the author chose this point of view?

   _____

   _____

   _____

> **Answer the questions about one of Cody's chapters in *The Wanderer*.**

3. How could you tell that Cody is the narrator of this chapter?

   _____

   _____

   _____

4. How would one of Cody's chapters be different if it were told from Sophie's point of view?

   _____

   _____

   _____

Name _____

Prefixes *in-*, *im-*, *ir-*, *il-*

> In each sentence, there is a word that needs a prefix. Choose a prefix from the box that will complete the word and make sense in the sentence.

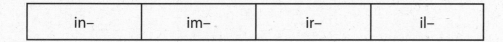

| in– | im– | ir– | il– |

1. It is _____polite to chew food with your mouth open.

2. The neighbors were worried that rats would _____fest the old, dirty house.

3. You do not need to wear fancy clothes to the _____formal dinner.

4. Unfortunately, the antique bracelet Toby broke is _____replaceable.

5. It is _____probable that we will win the game without our best player.

6. An _____logical idea probably will not work very well.

7. My sister has an _____rational fear of spiders and screams when she sees them.

8. John's sloppy handwriting was completely _____legible.

Name _____

Critical Vocabulary

> Read each sentence. Underline the sentence that best fits the meaning of the word in dark print.

1. usurped

The queen's cousin told lies to get her arrested, then he took over her throne.

Though the queen was cruel, her subjects willingly obeyed her.

2. banished

Please make yourself at home in our apartment.

I told my little brother to leave my bedroom and never return.

3. vanquished

I studied hard so I could do my best in the spelling bee.

The bus ride back to school was silent as the players thought about their defeat.

4. disposal

I never seem to have tissues with me when I need them.

I always make sure to have a notebook and pen with me so that whenever I have an idea, I can write it down.

5. mystifies

Though I enjoy football, the many rules confuse me.

I can explain anything you want to know about hockey.

> Choose two of the Critical Vocabulary words and use them in one sentence.

_____

_____

_____

Elements of Drama

A **drama** is a story that can be performed for an audience. Some elements of drama are **scenes**, **characters**, **dialogue**, **setting**, and **stage directions**.

> **Answer the questions about page 246 of** *Jason and the Golden Fleece.*

1. What information does the author share in the cast and prologue?

_____

_____

2. What is the purpose of these parts?

_____

> **Answer the questions about page 247 of** *Jason and the Golden Fleece.*

3. Throughout the play, what is the purpose of the italic text?

_____

4. Why is this information important?

_____

_____

> **Answer these additional questions about page 247 of** *Jason and the Golden Fleece.*

5. How does the dialogue reveal a problem or conflict?

_____

_____

6. What purpose does Storyteller serve in the drama?

_____

_____

_____

Prefixes in-, im-, ir-, il-

▶ Add a prefix (*in-*, *im-*, *ir-*, *or il-*) to the base words from the Word Bank. Write the word that best completes the sentence on the line provided.

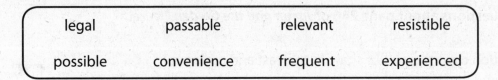

legal	passable	relevant	resistible
possible	convenience	frequent	experienced

1. When I saw the adorable kitten, I had a(n) _____ urge to pet it.

2. The hiker was clearly _____ , as he did not pack enough water and food for the hike.

3. Traffic came to a standstill after a landslide made the road _____ .

4. Snowfall is strange and _____ near the Texas Gulf Coast.

5. It is _____ to drive a motorcycle on a sidewalk.

6. People living on Saturn? That's _____ !

7. Our teacher reminded us to leave out _____ information in our summaries.

8. The doctor was running late with his appointments, and the receptionist apologized for the _____ .

Name _____

Critical Vocabulary

> Read each sentence. Underline the sentence that best fits the meaning of the word in dark print.

1. descend

I watched the city get smaller as the plane soared into the sky.

It's cold this far up the mountain, so let's climb down a bit.

2. practicable

That bike costs at least a year's worth of babysitting money.

She has supplies and he has tools, so together they can build a treehouse.

3. undertaking

I don't mind reviewing your work, as checking numbers goes pretty quickly for me.

I put off cleaning my room for so long that it was a huge chore.

4. expedition

The explorers gathered the supplies they would need for the journey to study the new land.

The scientists were pleased with the result of their experiment.

5. civilized

The archaeologist found proof that ancient peoples had complex systems of transportation and government.

After a year in the city, it was a relief to spend a day hiking in the quiet countryside.

> Choose two of the Critical Vocabulary words and use them in one sentence.

_____

_____

_____

Figurative Language

Authors often use **figurative language**, such as metaphors and similes, in their stories. Figurative language can bring to mind a certain emotion or create another special effect.

> **Answer the questions about page 267 of *Sacajawea*.**

1. What is the purpose of the simile in paragraph 16?

_____

_____

2. What does this simile tell you about Clark's character?

_____

_____

> **Answer these additional questions about figurative language in *Sacajawea*.**

3. Find a simile in Sacajawea's writing that makes a comparison to something common in her life.

_____

_____

4. What feelings are called to mind by the figurative language Sacajawea uses?

_____

_____

5. In paragraph 44, how can you use context to determine the meaning of *pirogue*?

_____

_____

6. Of what importance is this word to the selection?

_____

_____

Name _____

Greek Root *log/logue*; Suffixes –ous/–ious

> Work with a partner. Using your knowledge of the root and suffixes, predict the meaning of each word. Then use a print or online dictionary to confirm or correct your predictions.

Root or Suffix	Word	Meaning
log	dialogue	
logue	monologue	
–ous	virtuous	
–ious	uproarious	
–ious	suspicious	

> Write a sentence for each word in the chart.

_____

_____

_____

_____

_____

_____

_____

_____

_____

_____

_____

_____

_____

Name _____

Author's Craft

Author's craft is the language and techniques a writer uses to create a one-of-a-kind story. **Voice** is the unique style in which the author tells a story. **Mood** is the emotion created. Careful **word choice** by the author helps to create a memorable voice and mood.

▷ **Answer the questions about page 265 of** *Sacajawea*.

1. How does Jean Baptiste Charbonneau make his voice come across in this section?

_____

_____

2. How would you describe the tone of this section?

_____

_____

_____

_____

▷ **Answer these additional questions about author's craft in** *Sacajawea*.

3. Write a sentence or two from the text that demonstrates Sacajawea's voice. How would you describe Sacajawea's voice and tone?

_____

_____

_____

4. How does the author develop William Clark's point of view on page 266?

_____

_____

_____

Name _____

Prefixes com-, con-

▶ Read each sentence. Choose a word from the chart to complete each sentence. Write the word on the line. After writing the word, circle the prefix.

com–	con–
compassion	connect
combat	conform
compile	concentrate
combine	confer

1. The two judges will _____ to decide on a ruling of the case.

2. The doctor will give me medicine to _____ my illness.

3. Angie felt _____ and delivered warm food to those in need.

4. Did you know that the new bridge will _____ the two highways?

5. Carlos will _____ a list of his favorite books.

6. You will think of the correct answer if you really _____ .

7. Robert refuses to _____ to the new dress code at school.

8. Can you _____ the different ingredients to make a meal?

Critical Vocabulary

> Complete each sentence using the best Critical Vocabulary word from the Word Bank.

muster	rafters	fleet	tread
peril	skirt	tranquil	belfry

1. A noisy family of squirrels made a nest in the _____ of the barn.

2. The cheetah is a _____ runner that can reach speeds of over 70 miles per hour and change direction easily.

3. Every six months, the church caretaker climbs up to the _____ to polish the bells.

4. That fox was in _____ after it fell through the ice on a frozen pond.

5. Maple trees _____ the southern edge of the wide meadow.

6. A _____ of soldiers gathered to prepare for the parade.

7. In the early morning, the _____ lake is as smooth as glass.

8. I knew from my brother's heavy _____ that he had worn his work boots in the house again.

> Choose two of the Critical Vocabulary words and use each word in a sentence.

_____

_____

_____

Name _____

Point of View

The **point of view** is another way of saying who is telling the story. Poems have a speaker who narrates from a particular point of view. Personal pronouns tell the reader which point of view the narrator is using: **first person**, **second person**, or **third person**.

> Answer the questions about page 280 of *Paul Revere's Ride.*

1. Who is narrating the events in the poem, Paul Revere or a speaker?

   _____

2. How do you know?

   _____

   _____

   _____

> Answer the questions about *Paul Revere's Ride* and the informational sidebar "The True Story of Revere's Ride" on pages 284–285.

3. From what point of view is the informational sidebar told?

   _____

   _____

4. Compare and contrast how the point of view affects the poem and the informational sidebar.

   _____

   _____

   _____

Name _____

Prefix *im-*; Latin Root *magn*

> Complete the chart by adding two other words that contain the prefix *im–* and two that contain the Latin root *magn*. Using your knowledge of this prefix and root, predict the meaning of each word. Then use a print or online dictionary to confirm or correct the meanings you wrote.

Prefix/Root	Word	Meaning
im–		
magn		

> Write a sentence for each word in the chart.

_____

_____

_____

_____

_____

_____

_____

_____

_____

_____

_____

_____

_____

Elements of Poetry

Elements of poetry such as **rhyme**, **rhythm**, **imagery**, and **line breaks** all contribute to the way a poem sounds when it is read silently or aloud.

> **Answer the questions about stanza 5 on page 281 of** *Paul Revere's Ride.*

1. Where and how does the poet use rhyming words in stanza 5?

    _____

    _____

2. What rhyme scheme can you identify in stanza 5?

    _____

    _____

> **Answer the questions about the audio recording** *Paul Revere's Ride.*

3. Identify cause-and-effect relationships within the poem.

    _____

    _____

4. What transition words or phrases signal changing actions that move the narrative forward?

    _____

    _____

> **Answer the question about stanzas 10–13 of** *Paul Revere's Ride.*

5. How does the poet use cause and effect in the last four stanzas of the poem?

    _____

    _____

Name _____

Prefixes com-, con-

> ▶ **Complete each sentence by writing the prefix *com*– or *con*– in the blank.**

1. We can _____fort the boy by sending a card to his hospital room.

2. Can you please _____municate your concerns to the pilot?

3. The _____sensus of the sailors was to head into the storm.

4. We will make a _____parative study of gorillas and orangutans.

5. The doctor was _____fident the surgery would be a success.

6. A dog can make a wonderful _____panion for a child.

7. _____structive feedback will help me with my book report.

8. The musicians will _____gregate in the lobby before the game.

Name _____

Figurative Language

Authors use **figurative language** to help the reader visualize what is happening in a text.

> **Answer the questions about page 283 of *Paul Revere's Ride*.**

1. What does the poet mean when he says "the fate of the nation was riding that night"?

_____

_____

2. What examples of personification does the poet include in stanza 10?

_____

_____

3. How does the personification affect the reader?

_____

_____

_____

> **Answer the questions about pages 280–281 of *Paul Revere's Ride*.**

4. How does the poet's use of figurative language in stanza 3 set the mood?

_____

_____

5. How does the poet use figurative language in stanza 6 to describe the wind?

_____

_____

Prefixes dis-, ex-, inter-

> In each sentence, there is a word that needs a prefix. Read each sentence. Choose the prefix from the box that completes the word and makes sense in the sentence. Write the prefix in the blank.

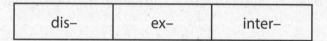

| dis– | ex– | inter– |

1. The baseball player _____located his shoulder.

2. The Olympics is a(n) _____national athletic event.

3. Our teacher granted us an _____tension on our homework due date.

4. We drove on the _____state highway from Florida to Texas.

5. Why do you always _____agree with everything I say?

6. I can tell by the _____pression on your face that you are surprised.

7. Rows of tomato plants were _____spaced with rows of zucchini plants.

8. The _____obedient dog refused to follow commands.

Name _____

Critical Vocabulary

You can use the words you learn from reading as you talk and write.

> Use details from the selection to complete the sentence stems below. Be sure to demonstrate the meaning of each Critical Vocabulary word.

1. Family courts will place a child with a **foster** family if

_____.

2. The **mission** downtown tries to provide help for people who

_____.

3. In order to understand someone's life, a **considerate** person will think about

_____.

4. The horrible destruction caused by a hurricane is a human **tragedy** because

_____.

5. The **wringer** on an old washing machine got rid of water in the clothes by

_____.

6. The audience felt **stricken** with fear while

_____.

7. Many couples today plan an inexpensive **matrimonial** ceremony, such as

_____.

8. After she twisted her ankle, her **gait**

_____.

> Choose two of the Critical Vocabulary words and use them in a sentence.

_____

_____

Name _____

Literary Elements

Characters are the people and animals in a story. **Setting** is where and when a story takes place. Characters' challenges and opportunities depend on where and when they live. Therefore, setting influences the choices they make.

▶ **Answer the questions about pages 304–306 of *Bud, Not Buddy*.**

1. How does the setting influence Bud's decision to lie?

_____

_____

_____

2. What do you learn about Bud's character?

_____

_____

3. What does the man mean when he says that "everybody's got a story"?

_____

_____

4. Why are the words *skinny* and *raggedy* in paragraph 13 good word choices?

_____

_____

5. Why do you think the author uses the word *folks* instead of *people* in paragraph 13?

_____

_____

Name _____

> **Answer these questions about pages 310–311 of** *Bud, Not Buddy*.

6. How does Bud's pretend family react to his presence at breakfast?

_____

_____

_____

_____

7. Bud's pretend brother sticks out his tongue at Bud after the meal. Why doesn't Bud respond?

_____

_____

_____

_____

_____

> **Answer these additional questions about** *Bud, Not Buddy*.

8. When Bud's pretend parents slap him, how does he react? How does that affect the plot?

_____

_____

9. When Bud realizes how far away Miss Hill and Chicago are, what choice is he forced to make?

_____

_____

Prefixes dis–, ex–, inter–

> Use what you know about the prefixes *dis–*, *ex–*, and *inter–* to choose the word from the Word Bank that best completes each sentence. Write the word in the blank.

| exhaustion | intercontinental | disinterested | interlude |
| disservice | excavation | interrogation | discolored |

1. After several washes, Lucy's new dress began to look faded and _____ .

2. If you don't get enough sleep and feel weak and confused, you may be

   suffering from _____ .

3. My mom asked me so many questions, it felt like a(n) _____ .

4. Except for a one hour _____ , during which students had a snack, the testing lasted all morning.

5. The loud and unruly behavior of a few fans does a great _____ to others who want to enjoy the game.

6. The museum offered a fossil _____ activity for kids.

7. She turned off the television because she was _____ in the election results.

8. Several airports offer _____ flights from North America to Europe and Australia.

Name _____

Suffixes –ence, –ance

The suffix *–ence* (meaning "an action or process" or "a quality or state") is found in words such as *intelligence* and *innocence*. The suffix *–ance* (meaning "an action, state, or quality" or "an amount or degree") is found in words such as *fragrance*.

> Complete the chart with other words that contain the suffixes *–ance* and *–ence*.

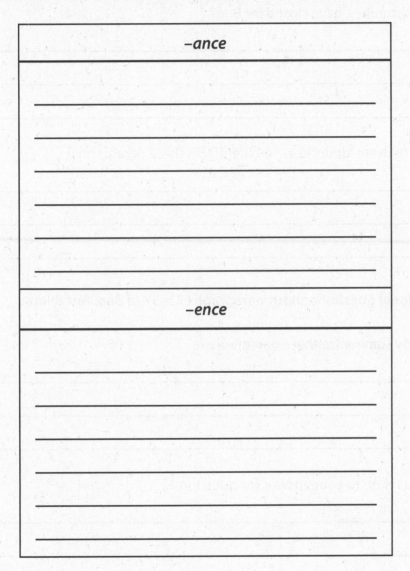

–ance
_____
_____
_____
_____
_____

–ence
_____
_____
_____
_____
_____

> Write a sentence for two words in the chart.

_____

_____

_____

Name _____

Theme

The **theme** of a story is its central idea, moral, or lesson. A story may have more than one theme. Themes may be stated directly or inferred by readers using evidence from the text.

> **Answer the questions about page 316 of *Bud, Not Buddy*.**

1. What "doors," or opportunities, have closed for Bud?

_____

_____

_____

2. What theme related to these "doors" can you identify in these paragraphs?

_____

_____

_____

> **Answer these additional questions about paragraphs 33–37 of *Bud, Not Buddy*.**

3. How would you briefly summarize these paragraphs?

_____

_____

_____

4. What theme can you relate to your answer for question 3?

_____

_____

_____

Name _____

Author's Craft

Author's craft includes **voice**, **mood**, and **word choice**, as well as **tone**, which is the attitude and feelings that an author or narrator has. Point of view, figurative language, and visuals all help to create the tone.

> **Answer the questions about page 314 of *Bud, Not Buddy*.**

1. What is the point of view, and what tone does it create?

_____

_____

_____

2. What does Bud mean when he talks about the "kind of dying that will make your eyes buck out of your head when you hear about it," and how does this description add to the story's tone?

_____

_____

3. What does the idiom "kicking the bucket" mean?

_____

> **Answer the questions about page 316 of *Bud, Not Buddy*.**

4. How does the author show Mrs. Rollins's and Bud's personalities in paragraphs 87–89?

_____

_____

5. How would you describe Bud's tone, or attitude, in paragraph 89?

_____

_____

Prefixes pre-, pro-

> Read each sentence and find the word that contains the prefix *pre-* or *pro-*. Write the word on the line, and divide the word after the prefix.

1. You should preheat the oven before putting in the casserole. _____

2. Careful driving can prevent many accidents on the road. _____

3. I was in the process of finishing my homework when the phone rang. _____

4. The history professor handed back our homework at the end of class. _____

5. The new computers increased our productivity at work. _____

6. Have you made a prediction about which team will win tonight? _____

7. Jenny was promoted to the position of supervisor. _____

8. Marcus knew about the party, but pretended to be surprised anyway. _____

Name _____

Prefixes *pre-*, *pro-*

▶ Choose the word from the Word Bank that best fits each definition. Write the word in the blank.

preregister	provision	previous	producer	preapprove
procrastinate	presentation	protection	preface	projector

1. _____ to sign up for a class in advance

2. _____ something meant to shield from possible danger

3. _____ to grant authorization in advance

4. _____ a machine that throws an image onto a screen

5. _____ an introductory statement

6. _____ to needlessly delay until a future time

7. _____ someone who grows agricultural products

8. _____ a speech made in front of a group

9. _____ a supply of food for future needs

10. _____ occurring beforehand or prior to

Name _____

Critical Vocabulary

> **Read each sentence. Underline the sentence that best fits the meaning of the word in dark print.**

1. deplorable

It's really admirable how much time she has devoted to helping other people.

She always speaks so rudely to her classmates.

2. downturn

Things were difficult at first, but our restaurant has really started doing well this year!

We need to figure out why the store is making less money lately.

3. abundance

We have to go to the store because we're going to run out of milk soon.

I'm always pleased that there are many different kinds of fruits and vegetables in the produce section of the supermarket.

4. graces

On my first day at the new school, he made me feel welcome by kindly showing me around.

As exam day approached, I hoped that I had prepared enough.

5. adversity

Their house burned down, and they didn't know what they would do.

We celebrated the end of another successful season for our team, as we had won all of our games.

> **Choose one of the Critical Vocabulary words and use it in a sentence.**

_____

_____

_____

Name _____

Media Techniques

Remind students that **media techniques** are tools that creators use to get their messages across effectively. They may include music and sound effects, narration, graphics, animation, and onscreen text.

> Answer the questions about the video *Stories of the Great Depression* on page 332.

1. What media techniques are used?

   _____

   _____

2. How is a video presentation different from print?

   _____

   _____

> Answer the questions about speakers in the video *Stories of the Great Depression*.

3. What details does a speaker share? How does this person's input add to your understanding of what life was like during the Great Depression?

   _____

   _____

   _____

   _____

   _____

   _____

   _____

   _____

   _____

Name _____

4. What is the person's name and where did he or she live during the Great Depression?

_____

_____

_____

_____

_____

Prefixes *intro-*, *im-*; Suffix *-able*

> Work with a partner. Using your knowledge of the prefixes and suffix, predict the meaning of each word. Then use a print or online dictionary to confirm or correct the meaning of each word.

Prefix or Suffix	Word	Meaning
intro-	introspective	
im-	impose	
-able	negotiable	

> Write a sentence for each word in the chart.

_____

_____

_____

_____

_____

_____

_____

_____

_____

_____

_____

_____

_____

Name _____

Content-Area Words

Content-area words relate to a specific topic. In a video, a viewer can figure out the meanings of these words by listening for context clues before or after the word. There may also be clues in the way a speaker looks or sounds when saying the word and in the onscreen visuals that appear at the same time as the word.

▶ Answer the question about content-area words in the video *Stories of the Great Depression* **on page 332.**

1. How is an electric light different from a "lamp light"?

_____

_____

_____

_____

▶ Answer these questions about content-area words in the video *Stories of the Great Depression*.

2. In the Chris Nix interview, what context helps you figure out the meaning of *deplorable*?

_____

_____

_____

_____

_____

3. *Deplorable* is derived from what base word? How are the meanings related?

_____

_____

_____

_____

Name _____

▶ Use your prior knowledge and experience to help you answer these questions about content-area words in the video *Stories of the Great Depression.*

4. How is a potbellied stove different from a cook stove? What do you think a potbellied stove might look like?

_____

_____

_____

_____

_____

5. *Crash* is a multiple-meaning word. Write three different definitions or sentences that illustrate the multiple meanings of *crash*.

_____

_____

_____

_____

_____

Name _____

Suffix –ion

> Read each sentence. Find the word with the suffix *–ion*. Underline the suffix.

1. Poison ivy can cause severe skin irritation.

2. Mr. Locke was happy to see our participation in the school play.

3. My father has a strong devotion to our family.

4. What is your prediction about who will win the game?

5. That factory is responsible for the production of fortune cookies.

6. The audience was interested in the demonstration of the new phone.

7. In your estimation, how tall is that mountain in the distance?

8. Put antiseptic on that scrape to prevent infection.

Name _____

Critical Vocabulary

> Complete each sentence using a Critical Vocabulary word in the Word Bank.

lax	vocational	rigid	ease	insisted
crusade	administer	perennial	improvised	

1. As chess club treasurer, it is my responsibility to _____ the club's money.

2. If you are too _____ about doing things your way, you will have problems making friends.

3. In the middle of the play, the actor forgot her lines, so she _____ them.

4. After eating two sandwiches and a banana, my hunger began to _____ .

5. Every summer, we enjoy our _____ trip to our family farm.

6. My cousin learned how to be a locksmith by attending a local _____ school.

7. Our teacher _____ that we clean out our desks before the weekend.

8. I tend to leave my things all over the house, so I guess you could say I'm

   _____ about picking up after myself.

9. Last week, a group of middle school students began to _____ for more vegetarian lunch options in the cafeteria.

> Choose two of the Critical Vocabulary words and use them in a sentence.

_____

_____

Name _____

Central Idea

Informational text generally includes a **central idea**, the idea that the text is mostly about. Individual paragraphs may have their own central ideas. The central idea is sometimes stated in the first or last sentence. Authors use evidence, such as facts and examples, to support the central ideas.

> **Answer the questions about paragraph 11 on page 341 of** *Children of the Great Depression*.

1. What is the central idea of this paragraph?

_____

2. What text evidence supports the central idea?

_____

_____

_____

3. How does this central idea fit into the overall theme of the selection?

_____

_____

> **Answer the questions about paragraphs 35 and 36 on page 350 of** *Children of the Great Depression*.

4. What is the central idea of these paragraphs?

_____

5. What evidence does the author use to support the central idea?

_____

6. Summarize this section, including only the most important information.

_____

_____

Latin Roots *migr, voc*

> Complete the chart by adding two words that contain the Latin root *migr* and two that contain the Latin root *voc*. Using your knowledge of these roots, predict the meaning of each word. Then use a print or online dictionary to confirm or correct the meaning of each word.

Latin Root	Word	Meaning
migr		
voc		

> Write a sentence for each word in the chart.

_____

_____

_____

_____

_____

_____

_____

_____

_____

_____

_____

_____

_____

Name _____

Text Structure

Text structure refers to the way writing is organized. Authors can use several different text structures, including **cause and effect** and **sequential order**. One of the most common text structures is **comparison/contrast**. In this form of organization, writers tell how different ideas, people, or things are alike and how they are different.

▶ **Answer the questions about page 344 of *Children of the Great Depression*.**

1. What text structure can you identify in paragraphs 21 and 22?

   _____

2. What transitional words or phrases signal this text structure?

   _____

3. How does this text structure improve readers' understanding of the selection?

   _____

   _____

   _____

▶ **Answer the questions about pages 343–344 of *Children of the Great Depression*.**

4. What comparison is made in paragraph 19?

   _____

   _____

5. What contrast appears in paragraph 20? What words signal that contrast?

   _____

   _____

Suffix –ion

> ▶ Read each sentence with a blank, and then look at the base word and suffix –ion listed below it. Write the base word with the suffix –ion added in the blank.

1. The lack of instructions caused some _____ among the students.
   Base word and suffix: confuse + –ion

2. Please submit a _____ of your essay.
   Base word and suffix: revise + –ion

3. What was your _____ of the new teacher?
   Base word and suffix: impress + –ion

4. James was in a state of _____ after the basketball game.
   Base word and suffix: exhaust + –ion

5. Are you in _____ of the missing library book?
   Base word and suffix: possess + –ion

6. Medicine helps with the _____ of many diseases.
   Base word and suffix: prevent + –ion

7. You can imagine my brother's _____ when he found the spider!
   Base word and suffix: react + –ion

8. Rosa needs _____ on how to build the model airplane.
   Base word and suffix: instruct + –ion

Name _____

Text and Graphic Features

Authors use **text features**, such as headings, introductions, and boldfaced words, to draw attention to specific parts of a text and to help readers find information. They use **graphic features**, such as photographs and diagrams, to explain ideas in a visual way or to add information related to the ideas in the text. Using a text and its features together helps readers gain a clearer or deeper understanding of the author's ideas.

▸ **Answer the questions about pages 339–340 of *Children of the Great Depression*.**

1. According to paragraphs 5–9, what was life like for children who worked during the Depression?

_____
_____
_____
_____

2. How do the graphic features support the text?

_____
_____
_____
_____

▸ **Answer these additional questions about *Children of the Great Depression*.**

3. What can you predict from the photo on page 337?

_____
_____

4. How do the text and graphic features on page 345 help you predict what the text is going to be about?

_____
_____

Name _____

▶ **Choose a graphic feature from *Children of the Great Depression*.**

5. How does the graphic feature help you better understand the text?

_____

_____

_____

_____

6. If you were to add another text or graphic feature, what would it be? What do you think it would add to the text?

_____

_____

_____

_____

Name _____

Word Parts

▶ **In each sentence there is a word with a suffix or both a prefix and a suffix. Read each sentence and underline the prefixes and suffixes. Write the base word on the line provided.**

1. We took our midyear assessment in math today.

   Root: _____

2. As of yesterday, no one has any clues about the man's disappearance.

   Root: _____

3. My art project is a creation using objects I found in my yard.

   Root: _____

4. Does Hannah sit directly in front of Aisha?

   Root: _____

5. I enjoy suspenseful movies that keep me on the edge of my seat.

   Root: _____

6. She asked her friend to make a recommendation on which sweater to buy.

   Root: _____

7. My doctor advised me to eat yogurt because it is light and digestible.

   Root: _____

8. I practice my speech every day, so my confidence has grown.

   Root: _____

Name _____

Critical Vocabulary

You can use the words you learn from reading as you talk and write.

> **Use details from the selection to complete the sentence stems below. Be sure to demonstrate the meaning of each Critical Vocabulary word.**

1. The law tries to live up to the **ideal** that

_____.

2. An increase in **productivity** at the charity car wash meant that

_____.

3. Some people think owning two cars isn't **extravagant**, but people on a tight budget might think

_____.

4. Health experts warn against the **consumption** of

_____.

5. If a person wanted complete **isolation**, he or she should

_____.

6. An Olympic champion might fail to **qualify** for a big race because

_____.

7. A judge in a courtroom maintains **objectivity** by

_____.

8. His parents offered him the **option** of doing what he wanted instead of

_____.

9. When it rains heavily for days, it often **induces**

_____ .

10. In order to **justify** what they've done, criminals will say

_____ .

▶ **Choose two of the Critical Vocabulary words and use them in a sentence.**

_____

_____

_____

Name _____

Central Idea

Nonfiction texts usually have a **central idea**, which is what the text is mostly about. The central idea can be identified by examining different parts of the text, such as headings, visuals, repeated words, and details. Details might include examples, facts, evidence, and description.

▶ **Answer the questions about pages 31–33 of *I Jumped at the Offer*.**

1. What is the central idea of the section "February 14, 1960" in paragraphs 72–91?

   _____

   _____

2. What text clues or details support the central idea?

   _____

   _____

   _____

▶ **Answer these additional questions about *I Jumped at the Offer*.**

3. How do the pictures and captions support the central idea of the section "February 14, 1960"?

   _____

   _____

4. What is the central idea of *I Jumped at the Offer*, and how is the section "February 14, 1960" connected to it?

   _____

   _____

   _____

   _____

Word Parts

> Read each sentence. Follow the instructions below the line to complete the sentence, and find the prefix or suffix from the chart that makes sense. Then write the word on the line.

Prefix	Suffix	
un– dis–	–ance –ment –able –ion	–ly –ation –ness

1. Upon closer _____ , I realized the brown object was a leaf, not a bug.
   Add suffix to base word *examine*

2. It is wise to present both sides of an _____ when writing an opinion essay.
   Add suffix to base word *argue*

3. The day at the lake was relaxing and _____ .
   Add suffix to base word *pleasure*

4. When the computer shut down _____ , I thought it had a virus.
   Add prefix and suffix to base word *expected*

5. The scared puppy walked with _____ as it explored its new home.
   Add prefix and suffix to base word *easy*

6. I saw my _____ in the water.
   Add suffix to base word *reflect*

7. The passenger who caused a _____ on the bus was asked to leave.
   Add suffix to base word *disturb*

8. Disapproval and _____ with city leaders led to a weak voter turnout.
   Add prefix and suffix to base word *enchant*

Name _____

Prefix de–; Suffixes –ion, –ism

The prefix *de–* (meaning "down," "from," "out," or "completely") is found in words such as *declare* and *destroys*.

The suffixes *–ion* (meaning "state of" or "condition") and *–ism* (meaning "the practice of" or "the system of") are found in words such as *presentation* and *heroism*.

> Complete the chart with other words that contain the prefix *de–* and the suffixes *–ion* and *–ism*.

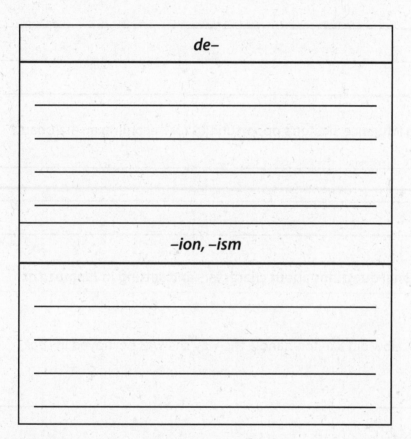

de–

–ion, –ism

> Write a sentence for each word in the chart.

_____

_____

_____

_____

_____

Name _____

Literary Elements

A narrative includes certain **literary elements**, such as **characters** and **setting**. In nonfiction narratives, the characters are real people, and the settings are real places. Setting influences the words, actions, and choices of characters.

▶ **Answer the questions about paragraphs 29–31 of** *I Jumped at the Offer.*

1. What do you know about Betty Skelton's character?

_____

_____

_____

2. How does the setting influence Skelton's opportunities for becoming an astronaut?

_____

_____

_____

▶ **Answer these additional questions about characters and setting in** *I Jumped at the Offer.*

3. Reread paragraph 31. How did Skelton handle the way she was portrayed in *Look* magazine?

_____

_____

4. NASA never considered Skelton as an astronaut candidate. How did this knowledge affect Skelton's actions?

_____

_____

_____

Name _____

Ideas and Support

Authors of nonfiction texts use **facts** to support their ideas. Readers should be able to identify facts and **opinions** so they can tell the difference between true statements and an author's personal beliefs.

▶ **Answer the questions about page 23 of** *I Jumped at the Offer*.

1. What opinion does the author present about women's lives during this time?

_____

_____

2. How does she support that opinion with facts?

_____

_____

_____

_____

▶ **Answer the questions about** *I Jumped at the Offer*.

3. What overall claim does the author make in this selection?

_____

_____

_____

4. What facts support this claim?

_____

_____

_____

_____

_____

135

Vowel Changes in Related Words

> **Read each sentence. Look at the underlined word. Look for its related word in the Word Bank and write it on the line.**

flammable	gravity	ignite	perspire
competition	negate	grateful	reside

1. The director was upset about the critic's <u>negative</u> review of his film.

_____

2. Joe wiped the <u>perspiration</u> from his face as he jogged along the beach.

_____

3. The apartment's <u>resident</u> was not home when we knocked on the door.

_____

4. Will you <u>compete</u> in the school games this weekend?

_____

5. After the accident in the schoolyard, Mr. Royko spoke in a <u>grave</u> manner.

_____

6. Harold showed his <u>gratitude</u> by making a card for his teacher.

_____

7. We saw the glow from a small <u>flame</u> deep in the dark forest.

_____

8. Marco turned the keys in the <u>ignition</u> to start the automobile.

_____

Name _____

Critical Vocabulary

> Read each sentence. Underline the sentence that best fits the meaning of the word in dark print.

1. implications

Because he was huffing and puffing after three minutes of running, we wondered if he had trained for the race.

The start line for the race is located near the entrance to the park, which is on Main Street.

2. aeronautics

The engineer checked over the plans for the boat.

Scientists figured out how to get the shuttle to fly.

3. priorities

It's more important to me to get good grades than to play computer games.

Sometimes I really don't care about practicing piano.

4. aloofness

I didn't understand why my neighbor ignored me when I waved to her.

My neighbor gave a friendly wave back when I waved to her.

5. engage

I decided not to enter the contest.

I took part in the science fair.

6. simulators

Pilots read the textbook to find out about the parts of an airplane.

Pilots used the machine to see what flying would really feel like.

> Choose one of the Critical Vocabulary words and use it in a sentence.

_____

Name _____

Point of View

Authors of nonfiction texts use first-person or third-person **point of view**. The **first-person** point of view uses personal pronouns *I* and *me*. This means that the author personally experienced the events detailed in the text. The **third-person** point of view uses the personal pronouns *he*, *she*, and *they*.

> **Answer the questions about** *Neil Armstrong: One Giant Leap for Mankind*.

1. What is the point of view in this selection, and why do you think the authors chose it?

_____

_____

_____

_____

_____

_____

2. How do the authors of this selection and the author of *I Jumped at the Offer* use point of view the same or differently?

_____

_____

_____

_____

_____

_____

Name _____

> **Answer the questions about paragraphs 30–32 of** *Neil Armstrong: One Giant Leap for Mankind.*

3. What event is described in this section? Who is describing the event?

_____

_____

_____

_____

_____

_____

4. What purpose does the quote in paragraph 31 serve by presenting ideas in a first-person point of view?

_____

_____

_____

_____

_____

_____

Name _____

Vowel Changes in Related Words

▶ Read each sentence. Select the word from the Word Bank that best completes each sentence and write it in the first blank. Write the related word in the second blank. Underline the vowel that changed its sound in the words. Not every word will be used.

collision	natural	division	reduction	serenity
conspiracy	relative	definition	knowledge	stability

1. Many foods today are made with _____ ingredients. _____

2. Icy roads from the snowstorm caused a car _____ . _____

3. Do you know the _____ of the word *aptitude*? _____

4. There was a _____ in the number of workers after the budget cuts.

   _____

5. Practicing balance is a way to increase physical _____ . _____

6. The equal _____ of chores among siblings is important. _____

7. My cousin Jeff is my favorite _____ because he likes to play chess with me.

   _____

8. After I read the book you recommended, my _____ of the American Revolution

   increased. _____

Name _____

Critical Vocabulary

> Read each sentence. Underline the sentence that best fits the meaning of the word in dark print.

1. **inevitable**

   There's no way to prevent it from raining.

   We can prepare by coming up with a second plan if it rains.

2. **module**

   The astronauts checked the dials and other readings to make sure everything was working.

   The astronauts prepared to separate the compartment from the rest of the ship.

3. **ascent**

   The airplane climbed higher.

   The airplane had a bumpy landing.

4. **legacy**

   She wrote books that people still learn from today.

   Unfortunately, all of the letters he wrote have been lost.

> Choose one of the Critical Vocabulary words and use it in a sentence.

_____

_____

Point of View

The **point of view** of a text describes how readers experience that text, either through a character in the story (**first person**) or through an outside narrator (**third person**).

▶ **Answer the questions about** *The Moon Landing Inspired Me to Become an Astronaut.*

1. From what point of view does the narrator write? How do you know?

_____

_____

_____

2. How does the author's perspective affect the way he relates the events?

_____

_____

_____

▶ **Answer questions about point of view in** *The Moon Landing Inspired Me to Become an Astronaut.*

3. Paragraphs 1–6 describe the author's experiences in 1969. What does he remember about that year?

_____

_____

_____

4. Paragraphs 7–10 describe the author's experiences as a space shuttle astronaut. How does the author feel about those experiences? What words tell you so?

_____

_____

_____

Name _____

Greek Roots cosmo, astro; Latin Root orbis

> Work with a partner. Using your knowledge of roots, predict the meaning of each word. Then use a print or online dictionary to confirm or correct the meaning of each word.

Root	Word	Meaning
cosmo	cosmic	
astro	astronomy	
orbis	orb	

> Write a sentence for each word in the chart.

_____

_____

_____

_____

_____

_____

_____

_____

_____

_____

_____

_____

_____

_____

Name _____

Author's Craft

The **author's craft** includes the language and techniques a writer uses to make his or her writing interesting to readers. The author's craft is evident in the **voice**, **tone**, and **mood** of a text.

> **Answer the questions about page 68 of** *The Moon Landing Inspired Me to Become an Astronaut*.

1. In paragraph 10, how would you describe the tone and mood as the narrator observes Earth from space?

_____

_____

_____

_____

_____

2. Explain what the author means in paragraph 11 when he says that traveling in the shuttle gives him a "unique perspective" of life.

_____

_____

_____

_____

Name _____

> **Answer questions about tone and mood in** *The Moon Landing Inspired Me to Become an Astronaut*.

3. Paragraphs 1–6 describe the author's memories of the year 1969. What is the tone of this part of the text?

_____

_____

_____

_____

4. How does the tone change in paragraph 8? How do you think the author feels about his role as an astronaut?

_____

_____

_____

_____

Name _____

Latin Roots

> **Read each sentence. Look at the underlined word and identify its Latin root. Write that root on the line.**

1. My mother will <u>transfer</u> to a new job on the other side of town.

   _____

2. My baby brother will be too much of a <u>distraction</u> at the movie.

   _____

3. Do these sneakers give you good <u>traction</u> on the basketball court?

   _____

4. The candidates will send us a new <u>proposal</u> about the cost of the designs.

   _____

5. We will meet in the <u>conference</u> room tomorrow morning.

   _____

6. Can you please sit on the <u>opposite</u> side of the table?

   _____

7. Please place the <u>disposable</u> razor in the trash.

   _____

8. To find the correct answer, <u>subtract</u> the smaller number from the larger number.

   _____

Name _____

Critical Vocabulary

> Complete each sentence using a Critical Vocabulary word in the Word Bank.

prohibitive	entice	enabling	venture	barriers
ordeal	colonize	mania	plague	anticipates

1. My sister is _____ me to improve my grades by helping me study.

2. Cleaning out your locker can be an _____ if you wait until the last day of school to do it.

3. Do doubts and worries _____ you the night before a test, or are you calm and cool?

4. If we are going to _____ another planet, we will have to find ways for humans to live there.

5. My cousin wants to sell rocks to tourists, but I don't think this is a good _____ .

6. The pizza restaurant is trying to _____ people to come in and eat by offering free dessert.

7. I think my neighbor has a _____ for plastic flamingos because he puts them all over his lawn.

8. The principal _____ that tomorrow's snowstorm will make the roads icy, so she has canceled school.

9. Shyness and a terrible singing voice are the _____ that keep me from joining the middle school chorus.

10. I'd like a new bike with a fancy paint job and a headlight, but I think the price will be

_____ .

> **Choose two of the Critical Vocabulary words and use them in a sentence.**

_____

_____

Name _____

Central Idea

The **central idea** of a text is what the text is mostly about. **Supporting details** tell about or support the central idea.

> **Answer the questions about page 77 of *Who Wants to Move to Mars?***

1. How would you summarize the main idea and purpose of this section of text?

_____

_____

2. How would you summarize details that support the idea that NASA is not interested in being in the business of space travel?

_____

_____

_____

_____

> **Answer the questions about the central idea in *Who Wants to Move to Mars?***

3. What important details support the idea that traveling to Mars would be difficult?

_____

_____

_____

4. Identify key words or phrases in the first three paragraphs that are clues to the text's central idea.

_____

_____

Name _____

Latin Root mit

> Complete the chart by adding three words that contain the Latin root *mit*. Using your knowledge of this root, predict the meaning of each word. Then use a print or online dictionary to confirm or correct the meaning of each word.

Root	Word	Meaning
mit		

> Write a sentence for each word in the chart.

_____

_____

_____

_____

_____

_____

_____

_____

_____

_____

_____

Name _____

Ideas and Support

Authors use **text evidence** to support their ideas in a text.

> **Answer the questions about paragraphs 17–19 of** *Who Wants to Move to Mars?*

1. What is the author's claim?

_____

_____

2. What support, or evidence, does the author provide for the reader that supports
this argument?

_____

_____

_____

> **Answer the questions about ideas and support in** *Who Wants to Move to Mars?*

3. What support, or evidence, is there for the statement, or idea, that you would need a
spacesuit to be outdoors on Mars for more than a few seconds?

_____

_____

_____

4. Read this sentence from the text: "There are so many reasons [for traveling to Mars] that
it is worth all the trouble." Is this an opinion or a fact? Explain your answer.

_____

_____

_____

Name _____

Latin Roots

▶ **Complete the sentence by writing the correct Latin root on the line.**

1. Be sure to de_____it your money in the bank.

2. What do you think is the pur_____e of this red button?

3. Flowers have bright colors that at_____ bees.

4. Which re_____ence materials did you use for your history report?

5. The bad news might de_____ from your chances to win the election.

6. The dentist will need to ex_____ the loose tooth.

7. You can improve your _____ture by standing up straight.

8. What in_____ence can you make about the character's motivation in the story?

Name _____

Author's Craft

You can strengthen your writing by using **rhetorical devices** such as **metaphor** (in which one thing is compared to another) or **personification** (in which an object is compared to a person). Writers sometimes use **logical fallacies** to make their writing appear stronger than it really is. For instance, they may appeal to nature or use the bandwagon fallacy.

> **Answer the questions about paragraph 27 of *Who Wants to Move to Mars?***

1. Which rhetorical device can you identify? Explain.

_____

_____

_____

2. What is the purpose of this rhetorical device?

_____

_____

> **Answer the questions about page 82 of *Who Wants to Move to Mars?***

3. Identify the logical fallacy in paragraph 30.

_____

_____

4. Why is this considered a logical fallacy?

_____

_____

_____

_____

Name _____

> **Answer the questions about author's craft in** *Who Wants to Move to Mars?*

5. Which rhetorical device is the author using in the phrase "a hostile planet" in
   paragraph 24? How do you know?

   _____

   _____

6. How is the team at Mars One creating a bandwagon effect, according to the author of
   the article?

   _____

   _____

Name _____

Latin Roots

▶ **Read each sentence. First, identify the word that has a Latin root and underline the root. Then write the meaning of the Latin root on the line provided.**

1. We went to the auditorium to listen to the class president give a speech.

   _____

2. The workers at the toy company manufacture dolls for children.

   _____

3. She often digresses when she speaks, making it difficult to follow her story.

   _____

4. The pilot had to eject himself from the airplane when the engine failed.

   _____

5. I asked the jeweler to add an inscription inside the ring.

   _____

6. She positioned the picture on the wall by her bed.

   _____

7. We squeeze the lemons to extract the juice when we make lemonade.

   _____

8. She had a vocation to become a doctor.

   _____

Name _____

Critical Vocabulary

You can use the words you learn from reading as you talk and write.

> **Use details from the selection to support your answers to the questions below.**
Then use the Critical Vocabulary as you talk with a partner about your answers.

1. What might you see in an underwater **realm**? _____.

2. What might an octopus do if a shark swims nearby looking for its **quarry**?

_____.

3. What is one question you would ask if you were **probing** into the habits of octopuses?

_____.

4. How could **manipulation** help you open a complicated lock?

_____.

5. Why might **classifying** marine life into specific groups be useful to scientists?

_____.

6. How might a loud boat cause a **disruption** if you were studying animals underwater?

_____.

7. What can you do if you find a certain topic **perplexing**?

_____.

8. What's the main difference between **mollusks** and fish?

_____.

9. What time of year do tree blooms usually **unfurl**?

_____.

> **Choose two of the Critical Vocabulary words and use them in a sentence.**

_____

_____

Name _____

Text Structure

Authors use **problem/solution text structure** when they want to identify and describe a problem and explain how it was resolved. They may use this pattern in a paragraph, part of a text, or the entire text.

Text Structure	Purpose	Signal Words
Problem/Solution	To show a problem and how it is solved	*problem, solution, in light of, propose, suggest*

> **Answer the questions about paragraphs 26–27 of** *The Octopus Scientists: Exploring the Mind of a Mollusk.*

1. What is the text structure of paragraphs 26–27?

_____

2. What problem is identified?

_____

_____

3. What solution is identified?

_____

_____

> **Answer the questions about paragraph 49 of** *The Octopus Scientists: Exploring the Mind of a Mollusk.*

4. What problem do octopuses face at the New England Aquarium?

_____

_____

5. How do octopuses solve this problem?

_____

_____

Latin Roots

▶ **Read each sentence. Choose the word from the Word Bank that best completes each sentence. Write the word in the blank.**

| progress | description | vocalize | attraction |
| manager | reject | inaudible | deposit |

1. My sister has been training to become a restaurant _____ .

2. The roller coaster is the main _____ at the amusement park.

3. The fans _____ their enthusiasm by cheering.

4. I am saving money to _____ into my new bank account.

5. Are you making much _____ on your science report?

6. The noisy airplane caused the child's voice to become _____ .

7. The grocer had to _____ the shipment of rotten produce.

8. Your poem has a wonderful _____ of the ocean.

▶ **Select a word from the box and use the meaning of its Latin root to help you write a sentence using the word.**

9. _____

   _____

Prefix octo–; Latin Root terr

> Complete the chart with words that contain the prefix and root.

octo–
_____
_____
_____
_____

terr
_____
_____
_____
_____

> Write a sentence for each word that you included in the chart.

_____

_____

_____

_____

_____

_____

_____

_____

Name _____

Text Structure

Authors use different **text structures** to organize information in a text. One type of text structure is **cause and effect**, which explains the connection between one event and another.

> **Answer the questions about paragraph 16 of** *The Octopus Scientists: Exploring the Mind of a Mollusk.*

1. In paragraph 16, what text structure does the author use to explain the reason why octopuses are so smart?

_____

2. How does the text structure help you understand the relationship between octopuses' intelligence and their lack of protective shells?

_____

_____

_____

> **Answer the question about the video** *The Camouflaged Octopus.*

3. What cause-and-effect text structure can you identify?

_____

_____

> **Answer the question about paragraph 22 of** *The Octopus Scientists: Exploring the Mind of a Mollusk.*

4. What causes an octopus to drill a shell instead of just chipping at it?

_____

Name _____

Author's Craft

Author's craft is language a writer chooses to convey mood and tone.

▷ **Answer the questions about paragraphs 7–10 of** *The Octopus Scientists: Exploring the Mind of a Mollusk.*

1. How does the author use first-person voice to convey her feelings and impressions?

_____

_____

2. What word choices convey mood and tone?

_____

_____

_____

_____

▷ **Answer the question about the video** *The Camouflaged Octopus.*

3. What tone does the narrator convey? Explain.

_____

_____

▷ **Answer the questions about other paragraphs of** *The Octopus Scientists: Exploring the Mind of a Mollusk.*

4. What word choices were specifically chosen to convey mood and tone?

_____

5. How do the mood and tone compare to the rest of the text?

_____

Name _____

Suffixes –ic, –ure, –ous

▶ **Read each sentence. Find the words that have the endings** *–ic*, *–ure*, **and** *–ous*.
Underline these endings.

1. We decided to hang the picture frame in the living room.

2. The girls laughed at the comic scene on television.

3. The crowd cheered as the famous musician walked onto the stage.

4. The wedding is a joyous occasion for the bride and groom.

5. The great white shark is a creature that lives in the ocean.

6. The elephant looks gigantic next to the tiny dog.

7. Agnes is jealous of her friend's ability to play the piano well.

8. The new factory will manufacture steel parts for trains.

9. The drama class gives an artistic performance in front of the entire school.

10. Riding your bicycle too fast down a steep hill can be dangerous.

Name _____

Critical Vocabulary

> Use details from *Poetry of the Sea* to support your answers to the questions below. Then use the Critical Vocabulary as you talk with a partner about your answers.

1. If someone described a riverside scene as **languid**, what would you think of?

_____

_____

2. How would you describe an audience's **receptivity** when a rock star takes the stage at a concert?

_____

_____

3. How would you dress if the temperature outside was **fluctuating**? Why?

_____

_____

> Choose two of the Critical Vocabulary words and use them in a sentence.

_____

_____

_____

_____

Name _____

Elements of Poetry

Elements of poetry include the structure and literary devices that a poet uses in a poem. Structural elements include line breaks and stanzas. Poets may also use literary devices, such as rhyme and imagery.

> **Answer the questions about the poem "Neither Out Far Nor In Deep" from *Poetry of the Sea*.**

1. In the poem "Neither Out Far Nor In Deep," which words create a rhyming pattern?

   _____

   _____

2. What effect does the rhyming pattern have in this poem?

   _____

   _____

   _____

> **Answer the questions about the poem "A Jelly-Fish" from *Poetry of the Sea*.**

3. What is the purpose of alliteration in line 3 of the poem?

   _____

   _____

   _____

4. What effect do the line breaks have in the poem?

   _____

   _____

   _____

Name _____

> **Answer the questions about another poem from *Poetry of the Sea*.**

5. How do the line breaks affect the rhythm of the poem?

_____

_____

_____

_____

6. How does the author use imagery, or words that create pictures in your mind, in the poem?

_____

_____

_____

_____

Name _____

Suffixes –ic, –ure, –ous

▶ **The words in the box end with one of the following suffixes: *–ic, –ure,* or *–ous*. Choose a word from the box that best completes each sentence. Then identify the word as an adjective or a noun.**

glamorous	composure	dramatic	infectious	spacious

1. The partners told the realtor they needed a _____ office for their growing company.

   adjective   **noun**

2. After a week of rain, there was a _____ increase in the number of frogs in our backyard.

   adjective   **noun**

3. The dog was sick with an _____ disease.

   adjective   **noun**

4. After being announced the winner, the candidate could not maintain his _____ and cried tears of joy.

   adjective   **noun**

5. At awards shows, movie stars wear fashionable and _____ clothing.

   adjective   **noun**

Name _____

Critical Vocabulary

You can use the words you learn from reading as you talk and write.

> **Use details from the selection to complete the sentence stems below.**
Then use the Critical Vocabulary as you talk with a partner about your answers.

1. An **organism** is any living thing, including

_____.

2. A marine biologist might **conduct** experiments to

_____.

3. Students might study marine **geology** to learn about

_____.

4. When you are **submerged** in the ocean, you are

_____.

5. To help save ocean species from **extinction**, you don't necessarily need

_____.

6. The main task of a fish and game **warden** is

_____.

7. Eugenie Clark's career in **zoology** was partly prompted by

_____.

> **Choose two of the Critical Vocabulary words and use them in a sentence.**

_____

_____

_____.

Name _____

Central Idea

A **central idea** is the big idea, or main idea, that readers should take away from reading a text. **Details** are small bits of information that support a central idea.

> **Answer the questions about page 132 of *Ocean Careers*.**

1. What central idea does the author present in this section?

_____

_____

2. What key details support this central idea?

_____

_____

_____

_____

> **Answer the questions about another section of *Ocean Careers*.**

3. What is the central idea?

_____

4. What key details support the central idea?

_____

_____

5. Write a brief summary of the section.

_____

_____

_____

Prefix sub–; Latin Root *hab*

> Work with a partner to complete the chart with words that contain the prefix *sub*–
and the Latin root *hab*. Using your knowledge of prefixes and roots, predict the meaning
of each word. Then use a print or online dictionary to confirm or correct
the meaning of each word.

Word part	Word	Meaning
sub–		
hab		

> Write a sentence for each word in the chart.

_____

_____

_____

_____

_____

_____

_____

_____

_____

_____

_____

_____

Name _____

Text and Graphic Features

Text features such as headings, introductions, and boldfaced words organize information for readers. **Graphic features** such as photographs, diagrams, and charts provide information in a visual format.

> **Answer the questions about page 135 of *Ocean Careers*.**

1. What does the mini-biography show and tell the reader?

_____

_____

2. How would you compare or contrast the information in the mini-biography with the information in the main text?

_____

_____

_____

_____

> **Answer the questions about pages 138–139 of *Ocean Careers*.**

3. What text and graphic features can you identify on these pages?

_____

4. What kind of information does each feature provide the reader?

_____

_____

_____

_____

5. How do the text and graphic features work together with ideas in the main text?

_____

_____

Name _____

> **Answer the questions about another section of *Ocean Careers*.**

6. What information do text and graphic features provide?

_____

_____

_____

_____

7. How do text and graphic features help readers better understand information in the main text?

_____

_____

_____

_____

Name _____

Prefixes de-, trans-

> In each sentence, there is a word that needs a prefix. Choose a prefix from the box that will complete the word and make sense in the sentence.

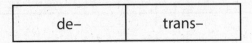

de–	trans–

1. We watched the climbers _____ scend from the summit of the mountain.

2. The packages were damaged in _____ it from the post office.

3. The scientists will _____ mit messages to the space station orbiting Earth.

4. The student _____ faced the textbook by scribbling on it.

5. Marie gave a tour to the new student who _____ ferred from another school.

6. Ms. Myers will _____ duct one point for each wrong answer on the test.

7. Can you please _____ flate the beach ball when we leave the pool?

8. My grandfather had to make several _____ actions at the bank.

Name _____

Critical Vocabulary

> Complete each sentence using a Critical Vocabulary word in the Word Bank.

pipeline	condense	via	respirators	
motivation	commission	opposition	proposal	oversees

1. The _____ carries gas to many homes in the city.

2. The librarian _____ a staff of ten student volunteers.

3. The student council wrote a _____ for extra recess time.

4. When steam cools, it will _____ into liquid water.

5. The governor expressed her _____ to the new policy.

6. My family traveled _____ train to visit relatives in California.

7. The _____ recommended that a new hiking trail be created.

8. _____ are very helpful to people who have difficulty breathing.

9. My best friend loves horses and has a strong _____ to learn how to ride them.

> Choose two of the Critical Vocabulary words and use them in one sentence.

_____

_____

Name _____

Text Structure

Informational texts organize ideas using a **text structure**. A **comparison/contrast** structure can be used to express advantages and disadvantages of an idea.

▶ **Answer the questions about paragraphs 5–6 of** *Safeguarding the California Coast.*

1. According to the text, what are the advantages and disadvantages of the pipeline?

   _____

   _____

2. How does the use of comparison and contrast help you understand why Erica spoke out against the pipeline?

   _____

   _____

▶ **Answer the questions about text structure in paragraphs 11–14 of** *Safeguarding the California Coast.*

3. What advantages and disadvantages did Erica have when she spoke before the California Land Commission?

   _____

   _____

   _____

4. What transitional words or phrases in which paragraphs signal a comparison/contrast text structure?

   _____

   _____

   _____

Name _____

Prefixes com-, con-

The prefixes *com–* and *con–* mean "with, together." The words **company** and **condense** contain the prefixes *com–* and *con–*.

> Complete the chart by adding words that begin with the prefixes *com–* and *con–*.

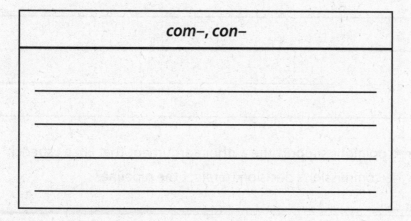

com–, con–
_____
_____
_____
_____

> Write a sentence for each word in the chart.

_____

_____

_____

_____

_____

_____

_____

_____

_____

_____

Name _____

Ideas and Support

Persuasive texts include **ideas and support** to persuade readers. Authors try to convince readers their ideas are correct by providing facts to support their claims.

▶ **Answer the questions about paragraphs 13–15 in** *Safeguarding the California Coast.*

1. What facts and opinions can you find on this page?

_____

_____

_____

_____

2. How do these facts and opinions support the author's argument that Erica's speech made a difference in the commission's decision to reject the pipeline?

_____

_____

_____

_____

▶ **Answer the questions about facts that support ideas in** *Safeguarding the California Coast.*

3. What fact about the cooling system of the pipeline does the author use to support her argument against the pipeline?

_____

_____

4. What fact about air pollution made Erica decide to fight against the pipeline?

_____

_____

_____

Prefixes de-, trans-

▶ Read each sentence. Choose a word from the chart to complete each sentence. Write the word on the line. After writing the word, circle the prefix.

de–	trans–
deflect	transcript
decode	transcontinental
decrease	transparent

1. The number of joggers at the park will _____ as we get closer to winter.

2. The secret agent was able to _____ the scrambled message.

3. The windows are _____ and allow light to shine through.

4. The soccer goalie used her hands to _____ the ball from flying into the goal.

5. The school will need a written _____ of Maria's grades.

6. The _____ railroad stretched across the United States.

Name _____

Author's Purpose

The reason an author has for writing a text is the **author's purpose**. Readers who determine this purpose can more easily recognize the author's message, or the main idea an author wants to communicate to readers. An author's purpose can be to inform, persuade, or entertain.

▶ **Answer the questions about page 152 of** *Safeguarding the California Coast.*

1. What evidence shows that the author wants readers to admire Erica's work?

_____

_____

_____

_____

_____

2. What is the author's purpose for writing this selection? Cite text evidence.

_____

_____

_____

_____

▶ **Answer the questions about another paragraph in** *Safeguarding the California Coast.*

3. What is the author's purpose in this paragraph? What does it tell you about the author's message?

_____

_____

4. Is the author trying to inform, persuade, or entertain in the paragraph?

_____

_____

Name _____

Greek Word Parts

> Read each description. Use what you know about Greek word parts to choose the word from the box that matches the description. Write the word on the line.

automatic	geologist	plutocracy	geomorphic
dermatology	democracy	sociology	thermostat

1. the study of skin and its diseases

_____

2. government ruled by the wealthy

_____

3. a person who studies the structure and development of the earth

_____

4. a machine that is self-operating

_____

5. the study of human beliefs, values, and interactions

_____

6. government ruled by the people

_____

7. a device that regulates temperature in heating and cooling systems

_____

8. pertaining to the shape of the earth

_____

Name _____

Critical Vocabulary

You can use the words you learn from reading as you talk and write.

> **Use details from the selection to complete the sentence stems below. Be sure to demonstrate the meaning of each Critical Vocabulary word.**

1. Many people enjoy smartphones because their **versatility** allows them to

   _____.

2. The **unprecedented** increase in college costs could not be anticipated because

   _____.

3. The house was **lavishly** decorated with the addition of

   _____.

4. The bare, open, and empty walls of the 1950s style house were **unadorned** with

   _____.

5. The silly **antics** of the class clown forced the teacher

   _____.

6. The **devotion** of the rock star's fans was obvious when they

   _____.

7. My father is a great mechanic who can keep an old **jalopy** running by

   _____.

8. A few people walking out of the mayor's speech turned into a **procession** because

   _____.

> **Choose two of the Critical Vocabulary words and use them in a sentence.**

   _____

   _____

   _____

Name _____

Literary Elements

Narrative nonfiction includes many of the same **literary elements** as fictional stories, such as **character**, **setting**, and **events**. Events are actions that happen in a narrative, and they build on one another and move a story forward.

> **Answer the questions about page 174 of *Babe Didrikson Zaharias*.**

1. What did Didrikson do after she failed to get on the girls' high school basketball team?

_____

_____

2. How did this event shape Didrikson's character?

_____

_____

> **Answer these additional questions about *Babe Didrikson Zaharias*.**

3. Using paragraphs 10–12 on pages 172–173, explain how the events about Didrikson's childhood help readers better understand her character.

_____

_____

4. Reread pages 183–184, paragraphs 44–47. Why is the final event at the parade important to understanding the story of Didrikson's life?

_____

_____

Name _____

Greek Word Parts

> Using what you know about Greek word parts, choose the word from the Word Bank that best completes each sentence. Write the word in the blank.

autonomous	meteorology	geochemist	zoology
monocratic	thermosphere	genealogy	aristocracy

1. Weather predictions sometimes seem like guesses, but _____ is a true science of Earth's atmosphere.

2. Solar activity affects increases in temperature in Earth's _____ .

3. Being independent is a trait of a(n) _____ person.

4. If you want to research your family history, consider using a _____ search engine on the Internet.

5. The British nobility, or _____ , declined due to social changes and high taxes.

6. Jayden is studying the composition of Earth and other planets to become

   a(n) _____ .

7. From the study of primates to the study of insects, _____ includes all analysis of animal behavior.

8. The emperor did not care what his people wanted and insisted on _____ rule.

> Write a sentence using one of the words from the Word Bank.

_____

_____

Latin Roots scrib/scrip

The Latin roots *scrib* and *scrip* (meaning "write") are found in words such as *describe* and *description*.

▶ Complete the chart with other words that contain the roots *scrib* and *scrip*.

scrib
_____
_____
_____
_____
_____

scrip
_____
_____
_____
_____
_____

▶ Write a sentence for three of the words in the chart.

_____

_____

_____

Name _____

Theme

The main message or lesson of a text is its **theme**. A theme might be clearly stated by an author, or it might have to be figured out using clues in the text. Narrative nonfiction, as well as fictional stories, can have themes.

> **Answer the questions about page 175 of *Babe Didrikson Zaharias*.**

1. After reading paragraphs 18 and 19, what might be the author's message or lesson?

_____

_____

_____

2. What details support this theme?

_____

_____

_____

_____

> **Answer these additional questions about *Babe Didrikson Zaharias*.**

3. What text evidence on page 174, paragraphs 15–17, supports the theme "never give up"?

_____

_____

4. Reread paragraphs 2–6 on pages 170–171. What message does the author give to future athletes through the telling of Didrikson's life?

_____

_____

_____

Name _____

Point of View

Point of view refers to how a story is told. Nonfiction texts may use **first-person** point of view, in which the narrator is a character and uses the pronouns *I* and *me*. Nonfiction texts may use **third-person** point of view instead, in which the narrator "disappears" and the pronouns *he*, *she*, *it*, and *they* are used.

▷ **Answer the questions about page 173 of** *Babe Didrikson Zaharias.*

1. What point of view does the author use in paragraph 13? Cite a sentence from the paragraph as evidence.

   _____

   _____

2. What point of view does Beatrice Lytle use in paragraph 14 when talking about her experience with Didrikson? How can you tell?

   _____

   _____

3. Why does the author give us Lytle's own words, rather than summarize what Lytle has to say?

   _____

   _____

4. Why do you think the author chose to write in third person instead of first person?

   _____

   _____

Greek and Latin Roots

▶ Read each sentence. Find the words that have the Greek and Latin roots *ped/pod, dent, voc, mort, man,* and *mem*. Underline these word parts.

1. You can improve your vocabulary through reading.

2. Julius Caesar will forever be immortalized in history books.

3. Use a pedometer to measure how many steps you took today.

4. Make sure to study the manual before taking the test.

5. Did you remember to turn off the television before you left this morning?

6. April visited the dentist after she cracked a tooth.

7. Use a tripod to steady the camera when filming your movie.

8. Make sure to be vocal at the protest march this weekend.

9. This factory manufactures parts for cell phones and tablets.

10. My uncle visited the podiatrist after he hurt his foot.

Name _____

Critical Vocabulary

> **Read each sentence. Underline the sentence that best fits the meaning of the word in dark print.**

1. impersonation

My dad laughed when I pretended to walk just like he does.

People often remark on how differently my father and I speak.

2. endure

After my second attempt to scale the wall, I gave up.

It was really hard to stick with the busy schedule, but I did.

3. unity

Even after hours of arguing, we couldn't come to an agreement.

We agreed to work together for the sake of everyone's well-being.

4. bicker

The children fought over the small toy.

The generous little boy offered half of his apple to a classmate.

> **Choose one of the Critical Vocabulary words and use it in a sentence.**

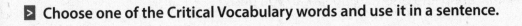

_____

_____

_____

_____

Name _____

Figurative Language

Authors use **figurative language** to make their writing more interesting and to help readers connect to what they are reading by visualizing the text.

> **Answer the questions about page 190 of *Sports Poetry*.**

1. What figurative language does the poet use in stanzas 1 and 2?

_____

_____

_____

_____

2. What does the figurative language help you visualize?

_____

_____

_____

_____

> **Answer the questions about page 192 of *Sports Poetry*.**

3. What examples of personification and onomatopoeia can you find?

_____

_____

_____

4. What effect does the figurative language have on the meaning of the poem?

_____

_____

_____

Name _____

> **Answer the questions about figurative language in *Sports Poetry*.**

5. What is the author comparing in the metaphor "my head, a carousel" in the poem "At the End of Warm-Ups, My Brother Tries to Dunk"? What does the author mean?

_____

_____

_____

6. What figurative language does the poet use in "Taking One for the Team," and what does it mean?

_____

_____

_____

Greek and Latin Roots

▶ Read each question. Use what you know about Greek and Latin word parts to find the best answer to each question. Write the word from the Word Bank on the line. Not every word will be used.

millipede	dentist	orthopedic	mortal	podium	memorandum
memorial	vocalization	biped	dentures	manicure	

1. What would you get if you want your hands to look nice? _____

2. Unlike humans, the gods and goddesses of Greek mythology live forever. What does

   that make humans? _____

3. What do you call a creature with more legs than a centipede? _____

4. What do you call a short business message? _____

5. Humans communicate with speech. What do dolphins use to communicate?

   _____

6. What kind of doctor would fix a broken wrist? _____

7. What might someone with missing teeth use? _____

8. What might an athlete stand on when receiving an award? _____

Name _____

Critical Vocabulary

> Read each sentence. Underline the sentence that best fits the meaning of the word in dark print.

1. diminish

I used to love playing tennis, but my interest has decreased recently.

My mom didn't understand the fuss about video games, but she really likes playing them now.

2. acknowledgement

Though I had my hand raised, my teacher did not notice me.

My teacher noted that I had asked an important question.

3. reinforced

We chose to install another lock on the door to increase our safety.

I chipped away at the lock, slowly getting it to break.

4. bribed

The official made promises in exchange for a large amount of money.

The politician promised to get the potholes filled and the garbage picked up on time.

> Choose one of the Critical Vocabulary words and use it in a sentence.

_____

_____

_____

_____

Name _____

Identify Claim

In an **argumentative text**, an author attempts to convince readers to feel a certain way or take a specific action. A **claim** is an author's statement of opinion on the subject of that text. An effective author supports each claim with **reasons** and **evidence**.

> **Answer the questions about paragraphs 17–21 of** *Who Gets a Trophy?*

1. What claim does the author make?

_____

_____

2. What reasons or evidence does he use to support his claim?

_____

_____

> **Answer questions about the section "Participation Trophies Send a Dangerous Message" on pages 202–203.**

3. What topic does the claim, stated in the title of this section, address?

_____

_____

_____

4. Does the author's claim solve a problem or answer a question? State the problem or question.

_____

_____

_____

Grade 6
© Houghton Mifflin Harcourt Publishing Company. All rights reserved.

Module 8 · Week 2

Name _____

Prefixes uni-, pro-

> Work with a partner. Using your knowledge of prefixes, predict the meaning of each word. Then use a print or online dictionary to confirm or correct the meaning of each word.

Prefix	Word	Meaning
uni–	unison	
pro–	proponent	

> Write a sentence for each word in the chart.

_____

_____

_____

_____

_____

_____

_____

_____

_____

_____

_____

_____

_____

_____

_____

_____

_____

Name _____

Ideas and Support

When an author shares an **idea and supporting evidence**, it is important to be able to tell a fact from an opinion. A **fact** can be proven true.

> **Answer the questions about page 203 of *Who Gets a Trophy?***

1. What opinion does Berdan express in paragraph 6?

_____

_____

2. What supporting evidence does she provide?

_____

_____

> **Answer the questions about pages 202–205 of *Who Gets a Trophy?***

3. How are Berdan's and Bugbee's claims the same? How are their claims different?

_____

_____

_____

_____

4. What support does Bugbee give for her reasoning?

_____

_____

_____

Name _____

5. Is her support fact or opinion?

_____

_____

_____

_____

> **Answer this question about** *Who Gets a Trophy?*

6. In paragraph 6, Berdan states, "I believe that we should change how we reward children."
Do you agree or disagree with her? Provide supporting evidence for your answer.

_____

_____

_____

_____

Name _____

Words from Other Languages

> Read each pair of sentences and look at the underlined word. Use a print or online dictionary to look up the word. Circle the answer that shows how the underlined word is pronounced.

1. Pasta is an Italian word. Pasta is a food made from flour paste, or dough.

        pä-stə   pā-stə

2. Umbrella is an Italian word. An umbrella provides protection from rain.

      ŭm-brĕ-yə   ŭm-brĕl-ə

3. Garage is a French word. A garage is an indoor place to keep your car.

      gə-räzh   gə-rĭj

4. Armada is a Spanish word. An armada is a fleet of warships.

      är-mă-dă   är-mä-də

5. Depot is a French word. A depot is a railroad or bus station.

      dē-pō   dē-pŏt

6. Tortilla is a Spanish word. A tortilla is a flat disk of bread, usually made of corn or flour.

      tôr-tē-yə   tôr-tĭl-ə

7. Dismiss is a Latin word. Dismiss means to send away.

      dĭs-mīs   dis-mis

8. Premiere is a French word. A premiere is the first performance of a play or movie.

      prĭ-mî-âr   prĭ-mîr

9. Monarch is a Greek word. A monarch is a king or queen of a country.

      mon-ərk   mōn-erk

Name _____

Critical Vocabulary

> Complete each sentence using a Critical Vocabulary word in the Word Bank.

cove	stationary	reputable	vaulting
radically	mechanisms	taut	obstacles

1. The hiker enjoyed _____ over the trees that had fallen across the trail.

2. There are small _____ inside my watch that make the hands turn.

3. The kayakers paddled around in the calm water of the _____ .

4. I purchased my new laptop from a _____ dealer who has been in business for a long time.

5. Yesterday was warm and sunny, but the weather changed _____ overnight, and today it is snowing.

6. The mountain biker had to ride around many _____ , such as trees and rocks.

7. A trampoline is made from a piece of _____ fabric that is stretched inside a metal frame.

8. The old train cars sitting on those tracks have been _____ for years.

> Choose two of the Critical Vocabulary words and use them in a sentence.

_____

_____

Name _____

Central Idea

Readers identify a **central idea**, or main idea, as they read to help them understand the text. Some informational texts are divided into sections. Each section has a main idea. Together, the section main ideas support the central idea of a text.

> **Answer the questions about page 216 of *Seven of the Wildest Sports Ever*.**

1. What is the main idea of this section?

_____

_____

_____

2. How does the main idea of this section support the central idea of the whole text?

_____

_____

> **Answer these questions about the section "Highlining" on page 219 of *Seven of the Wildest Sports Ever*.**

3. Which sentence in this section states the main idea?

_____

_____

_____

4. How does that main idea from the section contribute to the central idea and the author's main purpose for writing this selection?

_____

_____

_____

Name _____

Prefix *multi*–; Latin Root *man*

> Complete the chart by adding two words that contain the prefix *multi*– and two that contain the Latin root *man*. Using your knowledge of these word parts, predict the meaning of each word. Then use a print or online dictionary to confirm or correct the meaning of each word.

Word Part	Word	Meaning
multi–		
man		

> Write a sentence for each word in the chart.

_____

_____

_____

_____

_____

_____

_____

_____

_____

_____

_____

Name _____

Author's Craft

Authors use different techniques to make sure they communicate their ideas clearly. Authors' **word choice** and other elements create a **voice**, or style, that lets readers experience the author's personality. By using certain words and phrases, the author establishes a **mood**, or feeling, for the readers.

▶ **Answer the questions about page 215 of *Seven of the Wildest Sports Ever*.**

1. How would you describe the author's voice in paragraph 6?

_____

_____

2. In paragraph 9, what is the effect of the words *enthusiasts, creative, cooler,* and *exciting* on the reader?

_____

_____

▶ **Answer the questions about page 219 of *Seven of the Wildest Sports Ever*.**

3. What is the intended effect of "Don't try this at home!" in the caption?

_____

_____

4. How would you describe the author's voice in paragraph 26?

_____

_____

Name _____

Words with Silent Letters

> Read each sentence. Underline the word that has a silent letter and write the silent letter on the line provided.

1. If you could take only one book to a deserted island, which one would you choose?

_____

2. A rooster's comb, which is soft and smooth, helps the bird stay cool.

_____

3. I could not remove my ring because my knuckle was swollen.

_____

4. When we entered the empty house, the hair on the back of my neck bristled.

_____

5. Mario is still deciding what to do for his science project.

_____

6. We love to visit Colorado in the autumn when the leaves are turning colors.

_____

7. My aunt can speak three foreign languages fluently.

_____

8. My sister's favorite ballet is *The Nutcracker*.

_____

Name _____

Critical Vocabulary

You can use the words you learn from reading as you talk and write.

▶ **Use details from the selection to complete the sentence stems below. Be sure to demonstrate the meaning of the Critical Vocabulary word.**

1. The **excavator** on the scientific team approached the ruins and

_____.

2. The scientists put plaster over the **imprints** in the mud in order to

_____.

3. The doctors could tell the injured worker was in **agony** because

_____.

4. The sun setting over the ruins created a **dramatic** scene that showed

_____.

5. To make money, the people in the village **reproduced** some of the original

_____.

6. **Volcanic** rock comes from _____.

7. A **considerable** amount of effort is needed to

_____.

▶ **Choose two of the Critical Vocabulary words and use them in a sentence.**

_____

_____

_____

_____

_____

Name _____

Central Idea

The **central idea** of a text is the main idea of the text, or what the text is mostly about. Paragraphs and sections of texts may each have a central idea that supports the central idea of the overall text. Supporting details, such as facts and examples, provide the information the author wants readers to know about the central idea.

> **Answer the questions about paragraphs 1–10 of** *Bodies from the Ash*.

1. What is the central idea of this section of the text?

   _____

   _____

2. Which details in this section support the central idea?

   _____

   _____

   _____

3. Write a brief summary of these paragraphs, including a main idea and supporting details.

   _____

   _____

> **Answer the question about pages 244–245 of** *Bodies from the Ash*.

4. What is the central idea for the text on pages 244–245?

   _____

   _____

Name _____

> **Answer the questions about paragraphs 23–29 of *Bodies from the Ash*.**

5. In your own words, write the central idea of this section.

_____

_____

6. How does the author use examples as supporting details?

_____

_____

Name _____

Words with Silent Letters

> Read each sentence. Choose the word from the box that best completes each sentence. Write the word in the blank. Then identify the silent letters on the line below.

receipt	jostle	campaign	doorknobs
condemn	honesty	highest	edging

1. Joan climbed the _____ mountain in our state last year.

   _____

2. You can return your purchase if you remember to keep the _____ .

   _____

3. The king will _____ rebellious actions taken against his kingdom.

   _____

4. When I _____ a box of dog treats, my puppy comes running.

   _____

5. Most employers value loyalty and _____ .

   _____

6. The doors in the old house featured beautiful glass _____ .

   _____

7. My mom uses a metal garden _____ strip to keep weeds out of her garden.

   _____

8. Kyra, who is running for class president, asked me to be her _____ manager.

   _____

Name _____

Prefix ex-, Greek Root pyro

The root **pyro** has Greek origins. The meaning of the root **pyro** is "fire" or "heat." The prefix **ex–** (meaning "out of, from, or away") is found in words such as **excavator**, **example**, and **exit**.

> Complete the chart with other words that contain the root **pyro** and the prefix **ex–**.

pyro	*ex–*
_____	_____
_____	_____
_____	_____
_____	_____

> Write a sentence for each word in the chart.

_____

_____

_____

_____

_____

_____

_____

_____

_____

Name _____

> **Choose another photo in** *Bodies from the Ash***.**

4. What does the photo show? Paraphrase the caption.

_____

_____

5. How does the photo add to your understanding of the text?

_____

_____

Suffixes –ent, –ant

▶ In each sentence, there is a word that needs a suffix. Choose a suffix from the box that will complete the word and make sense in the sentence.

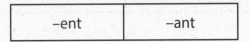

–ent	–ant

1. Mark felt insignific_____ standing next to the towering basketball players.

2. The defi_____ protestors marched to city hall.

3. The opposing baseball teams wore differ_____ uniforms.

4. Maya was a frequ_____ visitor to the comic book store.

5. Our dog is obedi_____ and follows all of our commands.

6. My brother was irritated by the professor's arrog_____ remarks.

7. James was reluct_____ to let me borrow his new bicycle.

8. After studying all night, Bryan was confid_____ he would do well on the test.

Name _____

Critical Vocabulary

> **Answer the questions below.**

1. Describe how a **chariot** in ancient times might have looked.

   _____

   _____ .

2. If someone built an **annex** to the place where you live, how would you use it?

   _____

   _____ .

3. What is an example of something that people might build a **shrine** to?

   _____

   _____ .

4. What subjects would a person need to study in order to perform an **autopsy**?

   _____

   _____ .

> **Choose one of the Critical Vocabulary words and use it in a sentence.**

   _____

   _____

   _____

   _____

   _____

   _____

   _____

Name _____

Text Structure

Text structure is the way an author organizes information in a text. Authors may use a **problem/solution** text structure to tell about a problem and explain how it is solved.

> **Answer the questions about pages 266–267 of** *King Tut: The Hidden Tomb.*

1. What problem did the Egyptologists want to solve?

_____

_____

2. What solution to the problem does the author explain?

_____

_____

_____

> **Choose other paragraphs of** *King Tut: The Hidden Tomb* **with a problem/solution text structure.**

3. What is the problem? What is the solution?

_____

_____

_____

4. What transitional words or phrases helped you identify the problem/solution text structure?

_____

_____

Suffixes -ent, -ant

> In each sentence, there is a word that needs a suffix. Choose a suffix from the box that will complete the word and make sense in the sentence. Then identify the word as an adjective or a noun.

-ent	-ence	-ency
-ant	-ance	-ancy

1. Marco was reluct_____ to open the door for the stranger. _____

2. A video provided compelling evid_____ that the defendant was guilty. _____

3. The radi_____ of her face told me that she had won the race. _____

4. Who will take Luis's role in the play if he is abs_____ tomorrow? _____

5. The colors add such vibr_____ to Sarah's paintings. _____

6. Sean was confid_____ that he had the right answer. _____

7. The store sells a variety of fragr_____ candles. _____

8. George Washington never lived in Washington, D.C., during his presid_____. _____

Name _____

Critical Vocabulary

> **Answer the questions below.**

1. What does a **profiler** observe as part of her job?

   _____

   _____.

2. What needs to be done when a person comes across a **homicide victim**?

   _____

   _____.

3. What happens to people's bodies on a hot day when there is high **humidity**?

   _____

   _____.

4. What is one way to change your **physique**?

   _____

   _____.

5. What is one place in the United States with high **elevation**?

   _____

   _____

> **Choose one of the Critical Vocabulary words and use it in a sentence.**

   _____

   _____

   _____

   _____

   _____

Central Idea

The **central idea** of a text is what the text is mostly about. Readers evaluate details in the text to determine the central idea. Supporting details can include examples, facts, evidence, and descriptions.

> **Answer these questions about paragraphs 24–28 of *Mummy Murder Mystery*.**

1. What is the central idea of *Mummy Murder Mystery*?

_____

_____

2. What details in paragraph 25 support this central idea?

_____

_____

> **Answer the question about *Mummy Murder Mystery*.**

3. Write a brief summary of the selection that includes the central idea and supporting details.

_____

_____

> **Answer these questions about page 275 of *Mummy Murder Mystery*.**

4. What is the central idea of paragraph 5?

_____

_____

5. How does the central idea of paragraph 5 support the central idea of the overall text?

_____

_____

_____

Name _____

Greek Root arch, Latin Root civ

> Work with a partner. Using your knowledge of prefixes and roots, predict the meaning of each word. Then use a print or online dictionary to confirm or correct the meanings of each word.

Root	Word	Meaning
arch	archaic	
arch	archaeological	
civ	civilian	
civ	civilized	

> Write a sentence for each word in the chart.

_____

_____

_____

_____

_____

_____

_____

_____

_____

_____

_____

_____

_____

_____

Name _____

Ideas and Support

In persuasive texts, an author may try to influence readers to think a certain way. The author states a **claim** and supports that claim with **evidence**. Readers must decide whether the author is stating a **fact** or giving an **opinion** to support the claim. A fact is something that can be proven. An opinion is a personal belief that cannot be proven true.

▶ **Answer these questions about paragraphs 21–22 of** *Mummy Murder Mystery*.

1. What is the author's claim for how the Iceman died?

_____

_____

2. What evidence supports this claim?

_____

_____

_____

3. How does the quote by Inspector Horn in paragraph 22 support the claim?

_____

_____

4. What facts and opinion does the author use in paragraph 23 to prove robbery was not the motive of the murder?

_____

_____

_____

Name _____

Suffixes –able, –ible

> In each sentence, there is a word that needs a suffix. Choose a suffix from the box that will complete the word and make sense in the sentence.

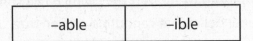

–able	–ible

1. Jenny knew that rain during the school picnic was inevit_____ .

2. Make sure to put the perish_____ food in the cooler before it spoils.

3. I find it irrespons_____ that you didn't finish your homework again.

4. His excuse for being late to school sounded cred_____ .

5. Do you know if these pretzels are ed_____ ?

6. Karla's new puppy is absolutely ador_____ .

7. According to the weather report, there is no snow in the foresee_____ future.

8. The museum display was access_____ to students of all ages.

Name _____

Critical Vocabulary

> Complete each sentence using a Critical Vocabulary word in the Word Bank.

atrophied	specimens	substantial	garments	contemplation
mutually	essential	halting	chaos	discernible

1. At the restaurant in Rome, the tourists spoke to the waiter in _____ Italian because they didn't speak the language very well.

2. Being friendly and being competitive are not _____ exclusive.

3. The patient's leg muscles had _____ after spending two weeks lying in a hospital bed.

4. The writer spent many hours in _____ before beginning her novel.

5. The old dress was faded, but the pattern was still _____ .

6. Archaeologists gathered arrowheads and other _____ from the site.

7. Many people believe that keeping lists is _____ for staying organized.

8. There was _____ on the playground when students rushed outside.

9. In summer, it's time to put away your winter _____ and find your shorts.

10. After a few months, the puppy's growth was _____ and we had to buy her a bigger bed.

> Choose two of the Critical Vocabulary words and use them in a sentence.

_____

_____

Name _____

Literary Elements

Literary elements are the pieces that make up a story. They include the characters and the setting. **Characters** are the people in a story. Authors develop characters by revealing what they think, do, and say. **Setting**, where and when a story takes place, may create conflicts for the characters and influence their choices.

▶ **Answer the questions about page 298 of *You Have to Stop This*.**

1. What do the characters' thoughts and words in paragraphs 107–111 reveal about the relationship between Cass and Max-Ernest?

   _____

   _____

   _____

2. How does the setting influence the plot of the story?

   _____

   _____

   _____

▶ **Answer the questions about the characters and setting of *You Have to Stop This*.**

3. What do Max-Ernest's jokes, skills, and actions reveal about his personality?

   _____

   _____

   _____

4. Describe the setting of *You Have to Stop This*, and explain how it affects Cass's choice to examine the mummy.

   _____

   _____

Suffixes –*ful*, –*less*, –*ence*

> Combine each of the following words with one or more of the suffixes. Use a dictionary to help you figure out which suffixes can be used with each word. Write down the meaning of each new word you create and its part of speech.

1. exist

_____

_____

_____

2. fear

_____

_____

_____

3. help

_____

_____

_____

> Look at each new word and its meaning. Write a sentence with each new word.

_____

_____

_____

_____

_____

_____

Name _____

Text and Graphic Features

Text features are special parts of a text, such as type styles, that call out something important. **Graphic features** are visuals, such as illustrations, that give information or support a text.

> **Answer the questions about paragraphs 20–21 of** *You Have to Stop This.*

1. How does the sign help readers better understand the setting of the story?

_____

_____

2. Why do you think the author uses different type styles in the sign?

_____

_____

> **Answer the questions below about** *You Have to Stop This* **and "Mummies: Milwaukee Public Museum."**

3. On page 289 of *You Have to Stop This*, the author includes a footnote about Boris Karloff. Why do you think the author uses a different type style for the footnote text?

_____

_____

_____

4. How do the print and graphic features of "Mummies: Milwaukee Public Museum" on page 300 affect how you think and feel about the mummies described in the poem?

_____

_____

_____

_____

Suffixes –able, –ible

> Read each sentence. Choose a word from the chart to complete each sentence. Write the word on the line. After writing the word, circle the suffix.

–able	–ible
dependable	plausible
agreeable	reproducible
advisable	indestructible
deplorable	collectible

1. Amy found a different hotel after she saw the _____ condition of the room.

2. The design is easily _____ in case you want extra copies for the class.

3. This rare 1938 penny is a _____ item that is sought after by many coin collectors.

4. Sam was _____ to joining his friends on the drive across the country.

5. The stunt driver felt confident and _____ as he rode his motorcycle around the track.

6. The only _____ explanation is that the raccoon tipped over the garbage can.

7. Do you think it is _____ to stand on the wobbly chair when changing the light bulb?

8. Stefan is _____ because he works hard and never misses a day of work.

Name _____

Elements of Poetry

Poets use a variety of elements to emphasize ideas and create effects in their poems. Poets organize the text of poems in **lines**, which are sometimes grouped into **stanzas**. Poems often include **imagery**, or the use of words and phrases to create mental pictures, or images, in readers' minds.

▶ **Answer the questions about "Mummies: Milwaukee Public Museum" on page 300.**

1. Find and interpret figurative language and imagery in stanza 131.

_____
_____
_____

2. How does the poem's structure support the meaning of the poem?

_____
_____
_____

3. How does the author's use of imagery help you visualize how the mummies walk?

_____
_____

4. Compare and contrast the topic of mummies in the text and the poem.

_____
_____
_____

Name _____

Homophones

> **Choose the correct homophone within the parentheses to complete each sentence. Write the word on the line.**

1. The airplane decreased altitude to begin its (descent, dissent) _____ for landing.

2. Did you know if you do not drive your car for months, and it sits (idle, idol) _____ , the battery may lose power?

3. Rick likes meaty (Chile, chili, chilly) _____ with very few beans.

4. The villagers convinced the brave knight to (slay, sleigh) _____ the dragon.

5. The trailer of the new movie really (peaked, peeked, piqued) _____ my interest.

6. What is the (capital, capitol) _____ of Nevada?

7. My salad is topped with golden (beats, beets) _____ , red onions, walnuts, and goat cheese.

8. (Wails, Wales, Whales) _____ is a country that is part of the United Kingdom.

9. The large ship had a difficult time sailing through the narrow (straight, strait) _____ .

10. During the jazz festival, the village was (teaming, teeming) _____ with people.

Name _____

Critical Vocabulary

You can use the words you learn from reading as you talk and write.

> **Use details from what you have read to complete the sentence stems below. Be sure to demonstrate the meaning of each word.**

1. An **activist** for student rights tries to _____

_____ .

2. The school places **restrictions** on the use of cell phones during exams in order to _____

_____ .

3. One of the duties of the members of the **clergy** is to _____

_____ .

4. New laws attempt to support the **abolition** of _____

_____ .

5. Students attend school to **obtain** _____

_____ .

6. Volunteers went house to house with **petitions** to _____

_____ .

7. In high school, you have to take notes during **lectures** because _____

_____ .

8. When the campgrounds **swarmed** with hornets, _____

_____ .

> **Choose two of the Critical Vocabulary words and use them in a sentence.**

_____

_____

Name _____

Literary Elements

Some texts include **literary elements**, including character, setting, plot, and events. In a biography, the subject is a real person. The setting is the time period in which the subject lived. The subject's internal traits and setting can affect the sequence of events in the subject's life.

▶ **Answer the questions about page 320 of *Why Couldn't Susan B. Anthony Vote?***

1. By describing Anthony's family, what does the author reveal about her internal traits?

   _____

   _____

   _____

2. Based on the details in paragraphs 8 and 9, how do you think growing up in a New England Quaker community in the 1800s affected Anthony's actions as an adult?

   _____

   _____

   _____

▶ **Answer the questions about page 324 of *Why Couldn't Susan B. Anthony Vote?***

3. What do Anthony's words in paragraph 20 reveal about her character?

   _____

   _____

   _____

4. How did being a suffragist during the mid-1800s affect Anthony's actions?

   _____

   _____

   _____

Name _____

Homophones

> Use context clues to complete each sentence. Write the word from the box on the line provided.

bazaar	waver	profits	vain	marshal
bizarre	waiver	prophets	vein	martial

1. People who think highly of their appearance or abilities are _____ .

2. Will all the _____ from the bake sale go directly to the charity?

3. The _____ in Morocco is a great place to shop for exotic rugs and spices.

4. Karate and kung fu are forms of _____ arts practiced for self-defense and physical fitness.

5. Modern _____ claim they can predict the future.

6. By signing a _____ , the farmer gave up his rights to the land.

7. When drawing blood, a nurse typically locates a _____ on the forearm.

8. Although the team was behind all season, the coach did not _____ from the plays he ran at practice each week.

9. Under the microscope, the bug looked like a _____ creature from outer space.

10. Our teacher invited the fire _____ to speak to our class about fire safety.

Name _____

Prefixes ex–, con–

The prefix **ex–** (meaning "out of, from, or away") is found in words such as **expected** and **extended**.

The prefix **con–** (meaning "with or together") is found in words such as **convince** and **consider**.

> Complete the chart with other words that contain the prefixes **ex–** and **con–**.

ex–	con–
_____	_____
_____	_____
_____	_____
_____	_____
_____	_____

> Write a sentence for each word in the chart.

_____

_____

_____

_____

_____

_____

_____

_____

_____

Ideas and Support

Authors of informational text use evidence, such as facts and other details, to support the **key ideas** they present in the text. The headings in an informational text can provide clues to the key idea in each section of text.

▶ **Answer the questions about pages 324–325 of *Why Couldn't Susan B. Anthony Vote?***

1. It is important for authors to give solid support for claims made in a nonfiction text. The subtitle for this section is "How did Susan B. Anthony fight for women's suffrage?" The author gives facts to support the subtitle and answer the question it asks. Name some of those supporting facts.

_____

_____

_____

_____

2. When her opponents criticized Susan and called her "devilish" and other names, what evidence did they have?

_____

_____

▶ **Read the section "Why was the Fifteenth Amendment so disappointing to the suffragists?" on pages 323–324 of *Why Couldn't Susan B. Anthony Vote?***

3. What is the key idea in this section?

_____

_____

4. What is a detail in the text that supports this idea? Explain how that detail supports the idea.

_____

_____

_____

Name _____

Author's Craft

Voice is the author's writing style that makes his or her writing unique. The precise words an author chooses create the **tone** of the text, or the author's attitude toward the subject or topic. The tone may be informal or formal, positive or negative, serious or humorous. The emotions a reader feels while reading create the **mood** of the text.

▶ **Answer the questions about the section "Why couldn't Susan B. Anthony vote?" on page 318.**

1. How does the author's choice of words affect the tone?

_____

_____

_____

2. What is the mood of this section? Explain your answer.

_____

_____

▶ **Answer the questions about paragraph 30 of *Why Couldn't Susan B. Anthony Vote*?**

3. What tone, or attitude, can you identify in this paragraph?

_____

_____

4. What mood is created by the last quote in the paragraph?

_____

_____

Name _____

> **Answer the questions about the section "Why did Susan's father take her out of school?" on pages 320–321.**

5. How would you describe the author's tone in this section of the text?

_____

_____

_____

6. What is the mood of this section? Explain your answer.

_____

_____

_____

Final –ary, –ery, –ory

> In each sentence, there is a word that needs a suffix. Choose a suffix from the box that will complete the word and make sense in the sentence.

–ary	–ery	–ory

1. The row of pine trees marks the bound_____ of our backyard.

2. Did you find the number for the front desk in the direct_____ ?

3. The principal has a the_____ about who left the gym doors open.

4. His story was a caution_____ tale about why you should be careful when riding your bike.

5. The princess showed great brav_____ when meeting the enemy soldiers.

6. We will pick up an apple pie at the local bak_____ .

7. We think that the tooth fairy is imagin_____ .

8. Sandy used trick_____ to get her dog to eat the medicine.

9. Your attendance at the band meeting is mandat_____ .

10. It is custom_____ to offer your guests something to eat when they visit.

Critical Vocabulary

> **Answer the questions below.**

1. Give advice for two people who are about to have a **confrontation**.

_____

_____

2. What is something that you have to **register** for in order to participate?

_____

_____

3. In your dream world, name a piece of **legislation** that you'd like to see pass.

_____

_____

> **Choose one of the Critical Vocabulary words and use it in a sentence.**

_____

_____

_____

_____

_____

_____

_____

_____

_____

_____

Name _____

Text Structure

Text structure is the way an author organizes the information in a text. An author may use a problem/solution text structure to identify problems and explain how they were or might be solved.

> **Answer the questions about page 338 of** *Turning 15 on the Road to Freedom*.

1. What problem is identified in paragraph 4 and how is it solved?

_____

_____

2. How does this text structure help you understand the struggles of African Americans during the civil rights movement?

_____

_____

_____

> **Answer the questions about page 341 of** *Turning 15 on the Road to Freedom*.

3. What problem is identified in paragraph 13, and how is it solved?

_____

_____

_____

4. How does this problem/solution text structure help you understand what the students experienced as they marched?

_____

_____

_____

Name _____

▶ **Answer these questions about problem/solution text structure in** *Turning 15 on the Road to Freedom.*

5. What is another example of problem/solution text structure in the autobiography?

_____

_____

6. How does the author help the reader understand the problems the marchers faced?

_____

_____

Name _____

Final -ary, -ery, -ory

> Choose a word from the box to complete each sentence. Write the word in the blank. Use each word only once.

memory	necessary	dormitory	visionary	shrubbery
obligatory	sanitary	mystery	cursory	snobbery

1. The college students lived in a large _____ .

2. My _____ is so good that I rarely forget anything.

3. We hid behind the tall _____ so the other team wouldn't see us.

4. My dad likes to keep our kitchen clean and _____ .

5. In many towns, it is _____ to wear a helmet while biking.

6. The school does not put up with bad attitudes or _____ .

7. We love it when our teacher reads an eerie _____ to the class.

8. Wearing sunscreen is _____ when you are at the beach all day.

9. He gave the report a _____ glance rather than reading it carefully.

10. Some Americans might call George Washington a _____ president.

Name _____

Critical Vocabulary

> Read each sentence. Underline the sentence that best fits the meaning of each word.

1. dignity

Even though I didn't win, I'm proud of the effort I put into the contest.
I'm still furious about the outcome of the competition.

2. denial

My mom gave me permission to go.
My mom won't let me go.

3. assaulted

He needed first aid for his injuries after the fight.
She thanked her neighbor for helping her fix the fence.

4. oppressed

In the early 1800s, it was illegal for many groups of people to vote.
The right to free speech helps to protect the press.

5. convocation

Only a few people have visited the moon.
The graduation ceremony will be held in the football stadium.

6. majesty

The sneaky rat scuttled underneath the garbage can.
The glorious eagle perched on the cliff at sunset.

> Choose one of the Critical Vocabulary words and use it in a sentence.

_____

_____

_____

_____

_____

Name _____

Ideas and Support

In persuasive texts, authors present a claim about a topic and try to **persuade** the audience to agree. Authors must support their ideas with solid **facts** and convincing opinions.

> **Answer the questions about page 350 of** *We Shall Overcome: President Johnson's Speech to Congress.*

1. What claim does President Johnson present to the audience?

_____

_____

2. How does President Johnson support his claim?

_____

_____

_____

3. Is this support for his claim a fact or an opinion?

_____

_____

_____

> **Answer the questions about the speech** *We Shall Overcome: President Johnson's Speech to Congress.*

4. How does listening to a speech help you understand important ideas in a way that is different from reading a speech?

_____

_____

_____

Name _____

> **Answer the questions about pages 352–353 of the text.**

5. What idea for improving voting rights does President Johnson present to the audience?

_____

_____

6. What facts does President Johnson use to support his idea for an amendment to the Constitution?

_____

_____

_____

Name _____

Review Greek and Latin Roots

> Work with a partner. Using your knowledge of prefixes and roots, predict the meaning of each word. Then use a print or online dictionary to confirm or correct the meanings of each word.

Root	Word	Meaning
voc	advocate	
civ	civility	
reg	regulate	
electro	electrify	

> Write a sentence for each word in the chart.

_____

_____

_____

_____

_____

_____

_____

_____

_____

_____

_____

_____

_____

_____

_____

Name _____

Author's Craft

An author's **voice** represents his or her style and personality. **Word choice** and other techniques establish a **tone**, or the author's attitude, toward a subject. The **mood** is the general feeling or emotions that the writing gives to the reader.

▸ **Answer the questions about page 349 of** *We Shall Overcome: President Johnson's Speech to Congress.*

1. How does the phrase ". . . for the dignity of man and the destiny of democracy" affect the tone?

   _____

   _____

   _____

2. Why is first-person point of view more effective here than third person?

   _____

   _____

▸ **Answer these questions about** *We Shall Overcome: President Johnson's Speech to Congress.*

3. Why do you think the president repeats the word "rights" twelve times throughout the speech?

   _____

   _____

4. What mood does his choice of words create in paragraph 26?

   _____

   _____

Singular and Plural Suffixes

> Read each sentence. Look at the underlined content-area word in each sentence. Under the sentence, write the singular or plural form of the content-area word.

1. Scientists read the three forms of <u>data</u> from the satellite.

Singular: _____

2. What do you think is the <u>basis</u> of Mark's opinion about your drawings?

Plural: _____

3. You are allowed to tour the school as an <u>alumnus</u> of the school.

Plural: _____

4. The sunlight streamed through the windows of the <u>atrium</u>.

Plural: _____

5. Please place the three <u>podia</u> back in the storage closet.

Singular: _____

6. The single <u>criterion</u> to be a member of the club is that you enjoy sports.

Plural: _____

7. My uncle in Arizona had three <u>cacti</u> in his backyard.

Singular: _____

8. Have you read the <u>synopses</u> of Eduardo's films?

Singular: _____

Name _____

Critical Vocabulary

> Complete each sentence using a Critical Vocabulary word in the Word Bank.

quavered	implored	political	scientist	polls
official	contrast	apathy	economist	fatigue

1. According to _____ baseball rules, the ball must be covered in white leather.

2. The parents _____ their children to study hard and make good choices.

3. The students showed _____ toward learning the rules of grammar.

4. A _____ may want to know why voters behave the way they do.

5. After playing a long game, the soccer players were overcome by _____ .

6. The student's voice _____ as he nervously began his oral report.

7. My parents go to the _____ early so they don't have to wait in line to vote.

8. The _____ studied changes in the stock market.

9. My sister never worries about anything while I, by _____ , am always nervous.

> Choose two of the Critical Vocabulary words and use each word in a different sentence.

_____

_____

_____

Name _____

Central Idea

The **central idea** is the most important idea in a text. In most texts, readers must infer the central idea based upon text clues and **key details** that the author includes in the text.

> **Answer the questions about page 366 of *Why Vote?***

1. What is the central idea about the role education plays in voting?

_____

_____

_____

2. What text evidence supports your understanding of the central idea?

_____

_____

_____

_____

_____

> **Answer the questions about pages 368–369 of *Why Vote?***

3. What is the central idea of paragraphs 30–32?

_____

_____

4. How does the quotation in large type on page 368 support this central idea?

_____

_____

Name _____

Greek Root *graph*; Latin Roots *duc*, **scrib/script**

> Work with a partner to complete the chart with other words that contain the Greek and Latin roots.

graph	
duc	
scrib/script	

> Write a sentence for each word in the chart.

_____

_____

_____

_____

_____

_____

_____

_____

_____

Text Structure

Text structure refers to the way a text is organized. **Transitional words** that authors use in the text can help readers recognize text structure. Authors may use one text structure to organize information in the text, or they may use more than one type of structure with a text.

> **Answer the questions about page 370 of _Why Vote?_**

1. What problem and solutions are cited in Donald Green and Alan Gerber's book?

_____

_____

_____

2. What transition words or phrases help you identify the text structure?

_____

_____

_____

> **Answer the questions about text structure in _Why Vote?_**

3. What section of text is organized within a problem/solution text structure? How can you tell?

_____

_____

4. Why do you think the author chose to organize this article using a problem/solution text structure?

_____

_____

Name _____

Singular and Plural Suffixes

▶ Read each sentence. Read the underlined content-area word in the sentence. Then write the singular or plural form on the blank below. If the sentence uses the singular form, write the plural form. If it uses the plural form, write the singular form.

1. The school's leaky roof caused a series of <u>crises</u> throughout the day.

   _____

2. The mushroom is one type of <u>fungus</u> found in moist areas.

   _____

3. Mr. Torres prints out a new <u>syllabus</u> every semester.

   _____

4. Make sure to include the report's <u>thesis</u> in the first paragraph.

   _____

5. The new sports complex included three <u>gymnasia</u> and tennis courts.

   _____

6. What are the <u>criteria</u> for selling goods at the school bake sale?

   _____

7. Hadley was the <u>focus</u> of attention at the middle school dance.

   _____

8. Stacy received an <u>aquarium</u> full of tropical fish for her birthday.

   _____

Name _____

Text Structure

Text structure is the way the information in a text is organized. Authors may choose to use one or many types of text structures within a text. If an author wants to explain events that happen and why they happen, he or she may choose to organize the information in a **cause/effect** text structure.

▶ **Answer these questions about page 364 of *Why Vote?***

1. What causes and effect does the author identify in paragraph 17?

_____

_____

2. How does this text structure support the author's purpose for the section "Why don't people vote?"

_____

_____

_____

▶ **Answer these questions about *Why Vote?***

3. What cause-and-effect text structure can you identify on page 363?

_____

_____

_____

4. Which of the causes, or reasons, described on page 363 as explanations for why people don't vote do you think is the most important for our government to address? Explain your choice.

_____

_____

_____

Vowel and Consonant Changes in Related Words

▶ Read each sentence and look at the underlined word. Circle the answer below that shows how the underlined word is pronounced. If you are unsure of the correct pronunciation, use a dictionary to look up the word.

1. Mirrors reflect light and images.

   rĭ·FLƏK   rĭ·FLĔKT

2. The reflection of the sun's rays off the lake was beautiful.

   rĭ·FLĔKT·sən   rĭ·FLĔK·shən

3. The product of 6 multiplied by 3 is 18.

   MŬL·tə·PLĬD   MŬL·tə·PLĪD

4. Do you know your multiplication tables?

   MŬL·tə·plĭ·KĀ·shən   MŬL·tə·plī·KĀ·shən

5. To prosper is to be fortunate or successful.

   PRŎS·pər   PRŎS·pĕr

6. A period of prosperity is a time of good fortune or success.

   prŏ·SPƏR·ĭ·tē   prŏ·SPĔR·ĭ·tē

7. The bicyclists rode at a rapid rate.

   RĂP·ĭd   RƏP·ĭd

8. The rapidity of the high-speed train was impressive.

   rĭ·PĬD·ĭ·tē   ră·PĬD·ĭ·tē

Vowel and Consonant Changes in Related Words

> Read each sentence and look at the underlined word. Circle the answer below that shows how the underlined word is pronounced. If you are unsure of the correct pronunciation, use a dictionary to look up the word.

1. The dancers performed with effortless grace.

GRĀS   GRĀSH

2. The hosts greeted their guests with a gracious welcome.

GRĀ•shəs   GRĀ•ses

3. A smoke alarm can detect small amounts of smoke.

dĭ•TĔK   dĭ•TĔKT

4. The early detection of smoke is important for fire safety.

dĭ•TĔK•shən   dĭ•TĔKT•shən

5. My eccentric neighbor takes his pet rabbit for walks on a leash.

ĭk•SĔN•trĭs   ĭk•SĔN•trĭk

6. That's not my neighbor's only eccentricity.

ĔK•sĕn•TRĬK•ĭ•tē   ĔK•sĕn•TRĬS•ĭ•tē

7. Please notify me if you know you will be arriving late.

NŌ•tə•FĬ   NŌ•tə•FĪ

8. I would appreciate the advance notification.

NŌ•tə•fĭ•KĀ•shən   NŌ•tə•fĭ•KĀ•shən

Name _____

Vowel and Consonant Changes in Related Words

▶ **Read each sentence and look at the underlined word. Circle the sound-spelling below that shows how the underlined word is pronounced. If you are unsure of the correct pronunciation, use a dictionary to look up the word.**

1. The wedding was a formal occasion.

   FÔR•məl   FÔR•măl

2. Due to the formality of the occasion, the groom wore a tuxedo.

   fôr•MƏL•ĭ•tē   fôr•MĂL•ĭ•tē

3. The family was curious about who was moving in next door.

   KYO͞OR•ē•əs   KYO͞OR•ē•ŏs

4. Their curiosity was satisfied when they met their new neighbors.

   KYO͞OR•ē•ŎS•ĭ•tē   KYO͞OR•ē•ƏS•ĭ•tē

5. She is an honest, fair, and moral person.

   MÔR•ăl   MÔR•əl

6. She is respected for her honesty and morality.

   mô•RĂL•ĭ•tē   mô•RƏL•ĭ•tē

7. As he delivered the sad news, he had a grave expression on his face.

   GRĀV   GRĂV

8. The survivors of the shipwreck realized the gravity of their situation.

   GRĂV•ĭ•tē   GRĀV•ĭ•tē

Vowel and Consonant Changes in Related Words

> Read each sentence and look at the underlined word. Circle the sound-spelling below that shows how the underlined word is pronounced. If you are unsure of the correct pronunciation, use a dictionary to look up the word.

1. I can taste the <u>acid</u> from the vinegar in the salad dressing.

   əS•ĭd   ĂS•ĭd

2. Vinegar has a high level of <u>acidity</u>.

   ə•SĬD•ĭ•tē   Ă•SĬD•ĭ•tē

3. We know that humans are <u>mortal</u> because they do not live forever.

   MÔR•tl   MÔR•tăl

4. The disease caused an increase in <u>mortality</u>.

   môr•TL•ĭ•tē   môr•TĂL•ĭ•tē

5. The annual <u>cycle</u> of the seasons is spring, summer, fall, and winter.

   SĬ•kəl   SĪ•kəl

6. The seasons recur in a <u>cyclical</u> pattern.

   SĬK•lĭ•kəl   SĪK•lĭ•kəl

7. The injured dog was taken to the animal <u>hospital</u>.

   HŎS•pĭ•tl   HŎS•pĭ•TĂL

8. The hotel staff welcomed guests with great <u>hospitality</u>.

   HŎS•pĭ•TĂL•ĭ•tē   HŎS•pĭ•TL•ĭ•tē

Name _____

Recognize Base Words

▶ Read the first sentence in each pair of sentences. Look at the underlined word and identify its base word. Write that base word in the blank in the second sentence of the pair. If you have difficulty identifying the base word, look up the word in a dictionary.

1. The book is about the colonists who founded Jamestown. Jamestown was the first

   permanent English _____ in North America.

2. Cats have great agility, which makes them good climbers and leapers.

   My _____ cat can leap from the floor and land on the kitchen counter.

3. The presidency of George Washington lasted for eight years. John Adams

   was _____ for four years.

4. A zoo is a place where you can observe animals in captivity. An aviary is an enclosure

   for _____ birds.

5. Salt water has a greater density than freshwater. Freshwater is less _____

   because it does not contain salt.

6. The intensity of the recent earthquake caused buildings to collapse.

   Less _____ earthquakes cause little or no damage.

7. Elitism is the belief that certain people are superior and deserve favored treatment.

   The word also refers to rule by members of the _____.

8. The drug company guaranteed the purity of the medicine. The medicine would be

   less effective if it were not _____.

Name _____

Recognize Base Words

> Read the first sentence in each pair of sentences. Look at the underlined word and identify its base word. Write that base word in the blank in the second sentence of the pair. If you have difficulty identifying the base word, look up the word in a dictionary.

1. The family took up <u>residency</u> in a new home. Family members hope to _____ there for many years.

2. A <u>libertarian</u> is someone who believes in free will. The word _____ means "the right to act as one chooses."

3. The lead runner's <u>complacency</u> caused her to slow her pace. She was so

_____ that other runners passed her.

4. A <u>diversity</u> of plants grows in the rainforest. Plants that grow in the rainforest

are _____ .

5. <u>Absolutism</u> is a form of government in which all power is held by one ruler.

In an _____ monarchy, the king or queen has all the power.

6. The <u>flutist</u> played a beautiful melody. He had been studying the _____ for many years.

7. The <u>economist</u> predicted the unemployment rate would decline. People believed her

prediction because she is an expert on the _____ .

8. <u>Delinquency</u> means "failure to do what law requires." A juvenile _____ is a person under the age of 18 who has broken the law.

Name _____

Recognize Base Words and Roots in Words with Absorbed Prefixes

> Read each word. Write the absorbed prefix and the base word or root on the lines. Then, read the definitions below and write the correct definition on the line.

Definitions	
to come together with violent impact	incapable of being moved
not fully grown or developed	to divide according to a plan
to go with as a companion	to set right
to fill sufficiently	to hold up

1. **correct:** prefix: _____ + root: _____

   definition: _____

2. **supply:** prefix: _____ + root: _____

   definition: _____

3. **apportion:** prefix: _____ + base word: _____

   definition: _____

4. **immature:** prefix: _____ + base word: _____

   definition: _____

5. **sustain:** prefix: _____ + root: _____

   definition: _____

6. **accompany:** prefix: _____ + base word: _____

   definition: _____

7. **immobile:** prefix: _____ + base word: _____

   definition: _____

8. **collide:** prefix: _____ + root: _____

   definition: _____

Recognize Base Words and Roots in Words with Absorbed Prefixes

> Read each word. Write the absorbed prefix, the base word or root, and suffix of each word on the lines. Then, read the definitions below and write the correct definition on the line.

Definitions	
not subject to death	not likely to be called to account
the act of communicating by mail or letters	making a strong mark on
a group of objects kept together	hanging by support to keep from falling
cannot be restored	something that is prohibited by law

1. **impressive:** prefix: _____ + base word: _____ + suffix: _____

   definition: _____

2. **collection:** prefix: _____ + root: _____ + suffix: _____

   definition: _____

3. **immortal:** prefix: _____ + root: _____ + suffix: _____

   definition: _____

4. **illegality:** prefix: _____ + base word: _____ + suffix: _____

   definition: _____

5. **correspondence:** prefix: _____ + base word: _____ + suffix: _____

   definition: _____

6. **suspended:** prefix: _____ + root: _____ + suffix: _____

   definition: _____

7. **irreplaceable:** prefix: _____ + base word: _____ + suffix: _____

   definition: _____

8. **irresponsible:** prefix: _____ + base word: _____ + suffix: _____

   definition: _____

Name _____

Recognize Roots

▶ Read each word. Write the prefix and the root of each word on the lines. Then, read the definitions below and write the correct definition on the line.

Definitions	
something gained	invasion, conquest, and control of a territory
a collection of things or people	a fond feeling toward another
impossible to make right again	period during which one owns or uses certain property
not inhabited	an attitude regarding anything flawed as unacceptable

1. **occupation:** prefix: _____ + root: _____

   definition: _____

2. **assortment:** prefix: _____ + root: _____

   definition: _____

3. **perfectionism:** prefix: _____ + root: _____

   definition: _____

4. **acquisition:** prefix: _____ + root: _____

   definition: _____

5. **unoccupied:** prefixes: _____ and _____ + root: _____

   definition: _____

6. **affection:** prefix: _____ + root: _____

   definition: _____

7. **irreparable:** prefixes: _____ and _____ + root: _____

   definition: _____

8. **occupancy:** prefix: _____ + root: _____

   definition: _____

Name _____

Recognize Roots

> Read each word. Write the prefix and the root of each word on the blank lines. Then, read the definitions below and write the correct definition on the line.

Definitions	
something designed to perform a specific function	The act or process of doing
to publicly declare one will no longer do something	reaching beyond the limits of recollection
one who makes public statements	Doing to be responsive
happening repeatedly	the act or fact of happening

1. **occurrence:** prefix: _____ + root: _____

   definition: _____

2. **announcer:** prefix: _____ + root: _____

   definition: _____

3. **appliance:** prefix: _____ + root: _____

   definition: _____

4. **interaction:** prefix: _____ + root: _____

   definition: _____

5. **reactive:** prefix: _____ + root: _____

   definition: _____

6. **recurrent:** prefix: _____ + root: _____

   definition: _____

7. **immemorial:** prefix: _____ + root: _____

   definition: _____

8. **renounce:** prefix: _____ + root: _____

   definition: _____